Food for the Future

T0087494

Food for the Future

Agriculture for a Global Age

JOSÉ BOVÉ AND FRANÇOIS DUFOUR

with a Foreword by André Coutin

translated by Jean Birrell

First published as Le Grain de l'avenir by Plon, 2002
This translation © Polity Press 2005

Polity Press
65 Bridge Street
Cambridge CB2 1UR, UK

Polity Press
350 Main Street
Malden, MA 02148, USA

Ouvrage publié avec le concours du ministère français chargé de la Culture – Centre national du livre.

Published with the assistance of the French Ministry of Culture – National Centre for the Book.

ISBN: 0-7456-3204-1
ISBN: 0-7456-3205-X (pb)

A catalogue record for this book is available from the British Library.

Typeset in 11 on 13 pt Scala
by Servis Filmsetting Ltd, Manchester
Printed and bound in Great Britain by
MPG Books Ltd, Bodmin, Cornwall.

For further information on Polity, visit our website: www.polity.co.uk

Contents

Foreword

The farming world, which was for a long time the only world, should not be allowed to lose its place at the heart of modern society. Many people today, however, have only a distorted view of it.

Living in cities, they are cut off from the realities of rural life, whatever the popularity of gardening, caravanning, doing up country cottages, rambling, nature parks, organic food, environmentalists, the bric-à-brac of our rural heritage, indeed of anything 'green'. When they are brought face to face with the land by natural catastrophes or food scares, they are confused and perplexed.

It is by no means easy to eat healthily, and not everyone knows how to eat well. To choose food wisely, you need a little knowledge and a lot of information. Good food is also part of our culture. Taste has to be acquired, and it can easily be spoiled if it is conditioned. Traceability is not necessarily transparency, and it can conceal certain parameters along the chain. As citizens, consumers are not free agents when they shop if they are not equipped to follow the public debate about farming and the issues that are shaping our way of life and the future of our society. The acronyms and the statistics, the administrative jungle, the lobbies, the fiefdoms and the private interests constitute an opaque screen that distances us from the realities and makes possible innumerable distortions and concealments of the truth. How can we decipher the jargon? How can we translate into plain language the discourse of technostructure and expose the lies of politicians and the special pleading of trade unions? The negative images and the stubborn misconceptions are distorting relations between city-dwellers and farmers and jeopardizing the chances of mutual understanding.

Who is best placed to lay the educational foundations of a reconstruction of farming? It could be José Bové and François Dufour, two men of the soil with deep roots in the countryside. A common struggle has prepared them to build for the future and to restore trust between farmers and citizen-consumers. They are of the same generation, and they are used to combining forces and pooling their complementary experience. José Bové, a sheep farmer, has experienced the revival of small farming in a countryside in decay, the creation of new enterprises and solidarity with farmers all over the world; François Dufour took over the family farm, at first practising intensive agriculture, then converting to organic farming. Both men are skilled communicators.

How did our paths cross? How did they and I meet? What made them talk to me? To answer these questions, I have to tell my own story, that of a young boy from Paris who immersed himself in the French countryside. In 1940, in an isolated village in the Massif des Maures, I saw cowpats drying in front of chalets; inside, I found cupboard-beds on the same floor as the cowshed. Back in the Île-de-France, during the years of rationing, I tried to produce my own 'farm' food. In an urban garden, I kept a few rabbits, and I ground grains of wheat in a coffee mill. In the kitchen, I made pasta with a rolling pin and cut it into thin strips to concoct my own version of noodles. After the war, in the French Alps, I climbed the peaks of the Tarentaise, where, in the mist, cowbells told where herds were grazing on the steep slopes. Another summer, when a storm beat down on the heights of the Vanoise, I took refuge in a cheese dairy and helped to produce Tome de Savoie by the traditional method. As an adolescent, I embarked on a bicycle tour of France, putting up in farmhouses along the way. As I climbed from the plains to the low mountains, I became aware of the diversity of agricultural production, and I saw how the conditions of peasant life changed, the gap in standard of living increasing with the altitude.

The cinema has never abandoned the land. But what really interests it is the villagers of *Farrebique* (1946) or *L'albero degli zoccoli* (1978; Tree of Wooden Clogs). There is a darker side to the picture, and it is becoming increasingly visible. Films that celebrate manual labour, nostalgia, and folklore can no longer conceal the revolt of an exploited work force. Harvest festivals and country weddings come and go, but are followed by the season of the 'grapes of wrath': the exodus from the country to the industrial suburbs, rural depopulation, and the many casualties of the technological revolution and victims of the 'glorious days' of agribusiness.

As a student in the aftermath of May '68 I read about the reoccupation of the Larzac plateau, the return to the land, and the first shoots of the pure, hard ecological movement, before its politicization. This was the time of the battle of the Loire, a river that is part of the European patrimony but under threat of canalization, and of the fight against all the cement manufacturers, planners, property developers and technocrats who are destroying the balance of the countryside and promoting an agriculture without farmers.

I became a journalist, and my research took me to Africa, South-East Asia, and Latin America. I immersed myself in the hurrying crowds of Tokyo, Cairo, Mexico, Hong Kong and New Delhi, but the people who lingered in my memory were those enslaved in the countryside rather than those imprisoned in the city: rice-growers in Thailand sculpting the mountain sides, Wolof market-gardeners in Senegal, sugarcane-cutters in Mauritius, aquafarmers in Japan, displaced Javanese in the forests of Borneo, Peul shepherds of the Sahel, olive-pickers in the Middle Atlas. As a reporter, I could hardly fail to notice that a third of the population was still rooted in the land. The world I saw remained populated by figures bowed down by toil.

It was the persistence of these images that led me to seek out José Bové and François Dufour, and carry our conversations well beyond the policies of the Confédération Paysanne, the radical farmers' union they founded in 1987. This book is in no way a manifesto for that organization. Its aim is to educate, to help people respond sensibly to food scares, and to restore confidence and solidarity in the world of living things.

There is a real need for a book of this type, one that proposes a new way of learning about farming as a family; a constructive way of looking at the countryside, of discovering local activities, of understanding biological life, of approaching wildlife without naive otherworldliness, of learning about the weather, of seeing how natural hazards may be prevented, of using one's powers of observation, of rehabilitating the concept of labour as a skill, and of seeing the produce of the land as having added cultural as well as economic value. To be ignorant of peasant memory and experience is to lack a culture. This book aims to make available to every citizen all the facts relevant to the great debate, the origins of the crisis, and the ways in which past errors can be avoided, and to enable them to pass on to their children something that is missing from their general culture, so that they will not be manipulated but will become active consumers.

That is why this book is a 'public service'. Our children can no longer be left in ignorance of our origins, of our deepest roots, and of the processes by which a post-industrial society has replaced a rural society. They ought to question us about the future that awaits them if we fail to safeguard the cultural values of our peasant heritage: knowledge, the transmission of ways of working the land, and a relationship with nature.

André Coutin

Glossary

AOC	Appelation d'Origine Contrôlée
BSE	Bovine Spongiform Encephalopathy, or mad cow disease
CAP	Common Agricultural Policy
FAO	Food and Agriculture Organization
FNSEA	Féderation Nationale des Syndicats d'Exploitants Agricoles (Farm Labourers' National Confederation)
GATT	General Agreement on Tariffs and Trade
GMOs	Genetically Modified Organisms
Groupama	Farmers' Insurance Company
JAC	Jeunesse Agricoles Chrétiennes (Young Christian Farmers)
MSA	Mutualité Sociale Agricole (farmers' social insurance scheme)
OECD	Organization for Economic Cooperation and Development
SAFER	Sociétés d'Aménagement Foncier et d'Etablissement Rural (Societies for Land Management and Rural Settlement)
WHO	World Health Organization
WTO	World Trade Organization

Map 1. *Farming in the European Community.*

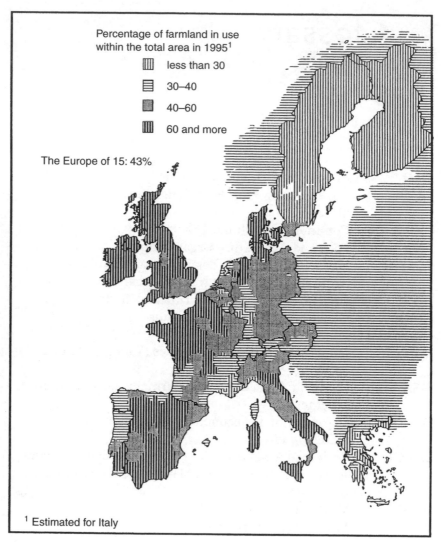

Sources: *Eurostat-NewCronos and Spanish government statistics. For Italy the percentage of farmland in use is an estimate.*

Map 2. *Small and large farms in France.*

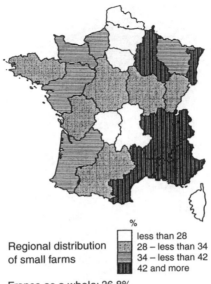

Regional distribution
of small farms

%
□ less than 28
▨ 28 – less than 34
▤ 34 – less than 42
▥ 42 and more

France as a whole: 36.8%

a. Farms of less than 10 hectares.

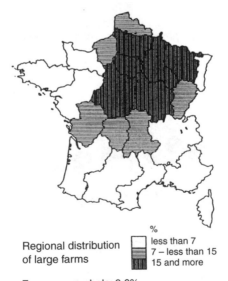

Regional distribution
of large farms

%
□ less than 7
▤ 7 – less than 15
▥ 15 and more

France as a whole: 9.6%

b. Farms of 100 hectares and more.

Source: *AGRESTE (1995).*

Map 3. Areas of major monocultures.

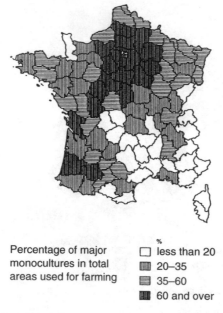

Percentage of major
monocultures in total
areas used for farming

%
□ less than 20
▥ 20–35
▤ 35–60
▦ 60 and over

Source: *AGRESTE (1995)*.

Map 4. Size of conventional farms partly converted to organic.

Area for farming
(in hectares)
80
40
8

■ organic
□ conventional

Source: *AGRESTE (1995)*.

Map 5. Concentration of pig production in France.

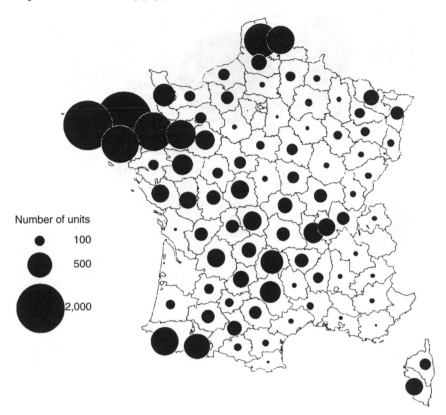

Map 6. *BSE in Europe: epidemiological situation in April 2002.*

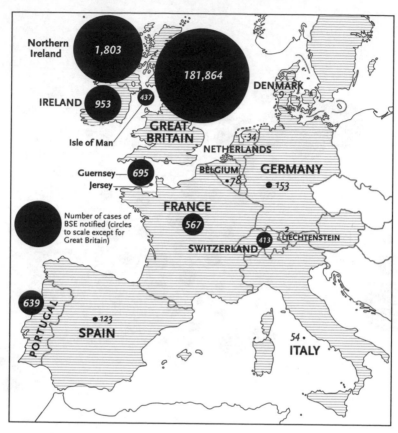

Source: *Office International des épizooties.*

Map 7. GM crop field trials.

Map 8. Protected zones in France.

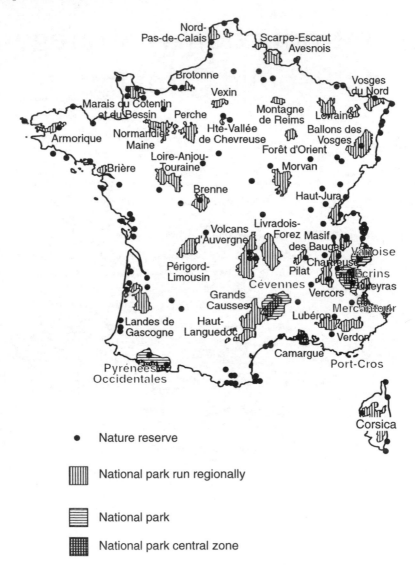

Nord-
Pas-de-Calais
Scarpe-Escaut
Avesnois
Brotonne
Vexin
Vosges
du Nord
Marais du Cotentin
et du Bessin
Perche
Montagne
de Reims
Lorraine
Armorique
Normandie
Maine
Hte-Vallée
de Chevreuse
Ballons des
Vosges
Loire-Anjou-
Touraine
Forêt d'Orient
Brière
Morvan
Brenne
Haut-Jura
Livradois-
Forez
Volcans
d'Auvergne
Masif
des Bauges
Vanoise
Périgord-
Limousin
Chartreuse
Pilat
Ecrins
Queyras
Cévennes
Vercors
Grands
Causses
Lubéron
Mercantour
Landes de
Gascogne
Haut-
Languedoc
Verdon
Camargue
Port-Cros
Pyrénées
Occidentales
Corsica

•   Nature reserve

National park run regionally

National park

National park central zone

Introduction: A Strategy to Rebuild Farming

Agriculture is like the glass that is either half empty or half full.

Reading the latest official indicators, the typical yuppie with a second home, or who weekends in the country, could easily believe that farmers are showing all the signs of prosperity.

The distressing images of piles of sheep burning in farmyards or of butchers deserted by their customers have quickly been forgotten; the foot-and-mouth epidemic, we are told, is over (only two notified cases); the consumption of beef has recovered to within almost 10 per cent of the level recorded before the fear of mad cow disease; pig and pork producers have benefited from the crisis. The safety of food in France, says the Minister of Agriculture, is an example to the rest of the world. As for French farms, they are well equipped and run by professionals who employ full-time wage-earners rather than seasonal workers.

In this rosy picture, the farmers of the year 2002 are younger than their predecessors, with a lower average age: 53 per cent are under 50, compared with 43 per cent twelve years ago. The farms of the third millennium are one and a half times bigger than those of 1988. Factory farming economizes on space and has freed up land for growing cereals.

It is all very reassuring for those who prefer to ignore the dark side of the picture. The reality is that it conceals a social tragedy, an ecological disaster, a critical health situation, and financial chaos. Yet, unless you walk around with your eyes shut, it is not difficult to see the failure of a Common Agricultural Policy that is a calamity for farmers, consumers and taxpayers, all citizens of a Europe that was promised the best of all possible worlds.

The confidence and the euphoria are based on a massive diagnostic error.

Those who run these enterprises, and win plaudits for their 'modernity', are no longer masters of their own farms and can no longer

1

choose how they farm. They are hopelessly overspecialized, and they are subject to directives and norms imposed from outside. They are employees of the food processing industry. The productivist system has ensnared them in long-term debt, and the banks exercise their control.

The increase in unit size has been achieved at the expense of small farms that practised diversification and multifunctionality. The technocrats hail the performance of farms managed by two or three partners. 'Look,' they say, 'the wives have been liberated from farm labour.' But do the loss of jobs and the disappearance of local craftsmen really constitute social progress and cultural enrichment? And where is the economic gain? Monoculture [see Map 3] makes these enterprises even more vulnerable to the laws of the market. Bankruptcy is a constant threat. And what is the advantage for the citizen? The methods employed are harmful to the environment and present an increasing risk to health.

The number of people employed in farming declines year on year; the rural population grows thinner on the ground, and the 'desertification' of the countryside proceeds apace. The soil is denuded, the water supply polluted, and the intensively reared animals are weaker and less protected against epizootic diseases. The farming community is divided by disparities in income, consumer confidence is eroded, and taxpayers complain about the demands of a subsidized agriculture. The jungle of regulations, the complexities of the new technologies, and the obfuscation of commercial strategies spread a smokescreen between responsible citizens and the farming world.

Cut off from reality, the citizen is kept in ignorance of rural life and is unable to appreciate the real issues or the nature of the future being stored up for our children by a handful of decision-makers.

The image of farmers is distorted by social tensions. Viewed from the towns, they look like subsidized malcontents, chronic polluters and occasional rioters; they belong to an untouchable lobby, they foment disorder, they are backward-looking, archaic and incapable of adapting to the world of the young.

They have too hastily been accused of fighting a rearguard action. On the contrary, they are engaged in constructive opposition in defence of values that have a future.

And they are no longer alone. They are part of a slow, unstoppable movement which can be called 'the awakening of the citizen', and which brings real hope. Civil society has decided to take charge of its own future; there will be no more blank cheques, no more tactical voting, no more 'political correctness'. All is not lost. The small farmers of Europe are a minority, but their voice has the support of a majority in civil society. An active minority is then capable of spreading the green revolution. A determined small group can spark a massive chain reaction that will be unstoppable. Social internationalism is responding to economic and financial globalization.

The weapons in the armoury of this peaceful movement are freedom of information and permanent debate. When citizens become agents in their own history, it is no longer possible to peddle untruths and pervert the judgement and opinion of the majority. Who, indeed, still talks of a minority? Small farmers may represent less than 4 per cent of the working population of France, but they are 60 per cent of the population of a world that is still rural. And the new awareness of the balance of power is worldwide. Agriculture is central to the debate; it determines the place people want to occupy on the planet they inhabit.

In the decades between 1945 and 1975, what the French call the 'Thirty Glorious Years', people were to be excluded from agriculture. In this mirage, farming was to be no more than a by-product of an automated industry quoted on the Stock Exchange. But farming needs men and women. Robots cannot replace them. The world in which our children grow up will be what we make – or let be made – of agriculture. To be modern is to anticipate and not to go on repeating the mistakes of the past, not lead people into the abyss like the flute-player of Hans Christian Andersen who charmed a whole village into following him into a river where they all drowned.

By attempting to denature agriculture, technostructure has demonstrated its inability to master the problem. The nature of things is regaining the upper hand. Civil society aspires to refocus itself around the fundamental activity of providing food. We are not, as a result, moving inexorably towards a pre-ordained slow death and the inevitable extinction of a minority activity.

For there to be a real dialogue between town and country, and for there to exist, at the level of the family, a common set of reference points and a body of basic knowledge, a multidisciplinary approach is essential. Without it, the real meaning will escape anyone who tries to decode labels, quality marks, instructions for use, and official advice, or who wishes to consume, vote and say 'yes' or 'no' in full knowledge of the facts. We need the help of agronomy, but also of history and geography, the life sciences and the human sciences.

We need an effort of memory, a new vocabulary, and a minimum of scientific baggage if we are to participate in a democratic debate relocating agriculture at the heart of a globalized society.

Cities continue to expand and contain an increasing proportion of the world's population. By 2000, there were fifty cities with more than ten million inhabitants. Modern cities have been built for the motor-car. You can drive for a hundred kilometres or more without seeing a field and without emerging from the interminable urban sprawl. Capital cities have lost their historic centres as they have spawned shopping malls and business parks. In the two Americas, in China and in Japan, linear urban monsters have developed along high-speed railway lines, gigantic concrete suburbs clustering round an ancient city. What can their inhabitants know of the rural world, even if it was the only world their ancestors knew? In today's industrialized countries, city-dwellers live cut off from the realities of farming life, however much they delude themselves by their leisure activities, their gardening or their weekend escape to their cottage, caravan, mobile home or houseboat. Doing up an old farmhouse is no way to learn about life on a working farm.

Staying in country cottages or walking in national parks, from the vantage-point of consumers, encourages the misleading notion of a nature created for leisure, that entertains its visitors with its quaint old villages and idyllic landscapes. A quick look through the shops selling country bric-à-brac and the obligatory visit with the children to the local open-air museum have the effect of burying farming life in a distant past, with forgotten rites, and Sunday best got out for a few folkloric festivals.

When there are storms, floods, forest fires, a drought, an epidemic or a mass outbreak of food poisoning, all that townspeople see on their televisions is a dramatized version of the catastrophe. The choice of images and the commentary are in the hands of intermediaries who lack basic knowledge and have no access to the true facts. They help to ensure that the public sees rural life through a distorting and reductive prism. Disasters apart, agricultural problems are mentioned only in connection with demonstrations embarked on by farmers driven to despair. Emotion gets the better of analysis. How can we understand a major crisis, or evaluate the possible remedies, if we know nothing of the origins of the tragedy, or fail to draw on the experience of the men and women on the ground? Television viewers have no way of getting a perspective on things when they are told about food safety, milk quotas, animal feedstuffs, BSE, foot-and-mouth disease or, above all, genetically modified organisms, if they lack a minimal scientific knowledge and basic practical experience.

We will never understand the problems that agriculture will pose for future generations unless we see them in the context of a long-term development, extending both backwards and forwards in time. The soil and the landscape are the product of thousands of years of labour and the transmission of a varied experience. We cannot predict or prepare for the future without a historical perspective. Ignorance of peasant memory exposes the citizen to the propaganda of the agribusiness lobby. Citizens have no guide enabling them to navigate freely through the jungle of the CAP or withstand the lies and manipulation. Globalization sets traps with words and with the ecological discourse it has adopted. Our book has the educational and democratic aim of equipping its readers to participate in a major debate from which they have too long been excluded and to become active consumers again.

1 Sites of Memory

By the 1930s, French rural life and village society had changed remarkably little since the eighteenth century. One in every two of the population lived in the countryside. Provincial France, with its 4 million farms, was still dependent on its network of sunken roads, and life was lived largely at the level of the canton. Most villages were within half a day's journey on foot of an administrative centre, and no one lived far from the corridors of power. The republican state relied on its peasant farmers and rubbed shoulders with them in the market towns and at local fairs and agricultural shows.

Just after the Second World War, what were French schoolchildren taught about peasant history? They were told about serfdom, the gabelle, the *jacqueries*, agrarian rituals, the lunar calendar, contacts and conflicts between château and village, the end of the feudal regime, the epidemics, the 'great scares', the 'republic of schoolmasters', Gambetta, and the Republic's dependence on its peasant farmers. Then, under the Occupation, its arable and its pastures were hailed as the life-blood of France, while its townspeople dreamed of eating fresh farm produce.

The first victory of the French peasantry was its accession to land ownership during the course of the nineteenth century. Some 38 per cent of farmers had owned only 2.5 per cent of the land. Managers and sharecroppers had worked on behalf of the owners of immense rural estates. Gradually, farm workers obtained plots and parcels of land. Under the Second Empire, living conditions improved, and the countryside became less isolated thanks to the arrival of the railways and the building of new roads. Mechanization had not yet reduced the size of the labour force. It has been seen as a golden age for those living on the land.

The Third Republic supported small landownership and gave the peasants social status.

In 1992, of a total of 53 million hectares of arable land, 45 million were privately owned, but it was not always the owners who farmed the land. In 2002, 10 per cent of farms accounted for 66 per cent of agricultural income, 50 per cent for a mere 5 per cent.

The massive rural exodus to the towns marked the twentieth century. It should not be forgotten, however, that this drift had begun in the century before, with emigration; there were 130,000 expatriates in 1865. It was at the end of the nineteenth century that René Bazin wrote *La Terre qui meurt*. In 1900, the number of peasants had fallen, but the eldest sons still stayed on the land. Increased productivity compensated for the reduction in the number of farm workers. Electricity reached even the smallest communes in the 1930s. The image of farms where everything was made out of wood, and where patriarchal families practised subsistence farming and relied on paraffin lamps for their lighting, was already anachronistic in the arable farming areas. Over a large part of the country, work on the land continued to support a number of other local trades. In the Lorraine village that was the birthplace of Fernand Braudel, there were nine craftsmen for every 200 inhabitants. Joiners, carpenters, cartwrights, blacksmiths, plough and wagon repairers, coopers, tilers, wool and linen weavers, saddlers, tinsmiths, basket-makers, clog-makers, well-diggers, mole catchers and water-diviners ensured that anything that was not done on the farm could be done nearby.

No geographer or historian would now dream of questioning the patient labour of the first peasants. Inhabitants of the *pagus*, the bourg and the canton, it was they who created – created, not improved – the French landscape. Some fifty years ago, the first aerial photographs revealed the mosaic of the ground below, with its bocage, open fields and clearings in the vast forests. Then, as you drove or cycled round the bends of a winding road, or crossed a river or a brook on a hump-backed bridge, or traversed the managed forests, or walked between the hedges of a sunken road, you appreciated the labour of previous generations and its diversity; you saw how they had adapted to the contours, to exposure, and to sun, shade, wind and rain, and how even the poorest and most barren soils had been put to use. Marshes had been drained, loess plateaux sown, stony hillsides terraced and planted with vines, and the richest soils turned into meadows. It was mixed farming that supplied these artists with their palette of colours. The tall silos mimicking those of the American West, the hangars that are prisons for pigs and factories for hens, the lines of high-voltage pylons, the motorways slicing through the countryside, the endless seas of corn, the Douglas firs and spruces, with never a broad-leaved tree in sight, the plastic greenhouses, the sewage farms, and the wastelands had not yet created the standardized, dismal plains of computerized monoculture.

During the 'Thirty Glorious Years', the mechanization of agricultural labour rapidly put an end to co-operative manual labour and reduced the number of workers on the land. At first, a generation of machines on a human scale improved farmers' living conditions. But increasingly powerful machines soon made their appearance on the market, responding to the gigantism of the largest farms. The tractor is to green Europe what the panzer was to the blitzkrieg.

The end of the Second World War did not mean the end of rationing. In the years of reconstruction, the Fourth Republic asked its farmers to ensure by their labour that the country was self-sufficient in food. Their collective efforts enabled them to succeed in fulfilling this mission on behalf of the nation.

Up to the 1960s, the sons of farmers who had remained on the land were able to see the family farm operating as a balanced unit in a village community that was assimilating the first mechanization and gradually modernizing. Those who had left for the towns were able to observe the transition from traditional extensive agriculture in small dispersed units to an intensive agriculture required to adopt the iron laws of industrialization.

In 1962, the farmers had fulfilled the task assigned to them, that of feeding the nation. They had believed in the progress that would liberate them. Had they not been taught since 1950 that, in the utopia of the Common Market, 'farming will no longer have to beg for the support of each state, but will prosper in the context of a united Europe'? This was the beginning of the break with reality and the natural order of things.

José Bové's grandparents were farmers. His father, Josy, left the family farm to study agronomy and then went into research. His work took him to the United States, where he spent three years.

By the time I was born, my mother and father already lived in a town. But my great-aunt had a little farm about fifteen kilometres from Bordeaux. When I was just a toddler, my parents used to take me to see her. The house had a kitchen garden alongside, a well in the yard, and a byre with four or five cows. These are the first images of the country that I can remember. But the expanding suburbs of Bordeaux soon reached the district, and it is now completely urbanized. No trace of the farm survives. All I have to remind me of this early childhood experience is a collar with a cowbell.

From the age of 3 until I was 6, I lived with my parents in the United States. My first images of intensive agriculture were the fields of California stretching as far as the eye could see. My parents' research work meant that they travelled extensively from our base in Berkeley. We crossed the great cultivated plains of the West, vast stretches of maize, oilseed rape and corn unfolding before my infant eyes. When I was 4 or 5, we went to Hawaii, and my most vivid memories are of the banana harvest. In the fields, the gathered fruits were piled on to conveyer belts, from which they were tumbled into the backs of enormous lorries. It was an open-air assembly line and my first image of a mode of production totally unlike subsistence farming.

Far from this mechanization, reading plunged me into a world of ancient agriculture. In California, I read and reread a book I loved, the story of a little Mexican peasant boy and his donkey. When I crossed the Mexican border with my parents, I discovered another way of life, where the villagers cultivated little plots of land and livestock wandered through the streets. Returning to the plains of California, I was surrounded by never-ending rows of fruit trees. Child though I was, struck by the extreme contrast between two types of agriculture and two ways of life, I made the connection between the old farm of my great-aunt on the outskirts of Bordeaux and those Mexican peasants separated by a frontier and light-years from the farmers of America.

When we returned to France, I went to visit the birthplace of my family, part of which came from Luxembourg. A distant relative had a farm and a small shop in a village. The two buildings were separated by a yard, and here, still a little boy, I played with the local children. We channelled the trickles of slurry seeping out of the dung heap into streams and built bridges over them. At the age of 7, I felt entirely at home on these little farms integrated into the village. A link was re-established that could never be broken; even if I moved away and even if I travelled, it would be my guiding principle.

On holidays in southern Germany and Austria, I was among the family farms of the mountains, where the cultivation of cereals was combined with pig farming. Meanwhile, even in Luxembourg, I had seen once again the contrast that had so struck me in the Americas between the land and the machine. In the few plains of the Grand Duchy, I had seen the first combine harvesters in operation. These monsters fascinated me. These days, they are no longer used.

So I absorbed as a very young child the image of a two-speed and almost schizophrenic agriculture: part on the scale of the family unit, part on that of the wide-open spaces, where machines were beginning to replace humans.

What I had found most striking and most important in the United States was the complete rupture between town and country. There was no contact between the two worlds. In the absence of such links, no construction or reconstruction of the countryside of the sort that has been conceived and developed in France was imaginable. In Europe, family ties, festive rites and culinary traditions survived; there were circuits and networks, and an interdependence of farmers, artisans and local shopkeepers. Everything was interconnected.

Two events, a catastrophe and a plague, gave me a glimpse of the natural risks to which rural life is particularly exposed but also well equipped to handle. During the first great forest fire in the Landes, in which some fifty people died, there was a resurgence of flames in the area where my great-aunt lived. In the battle against the fire, the villagers showed exemplary solidarity. Another example of mutual co-operation was the response of the inhabitants to an invasion of crickets. This was during the war, when my mother and maternal grandparents made frequent trips by bicycle to see my great-aunt. My mother described to me how the villagers had gone out *en masse*, beating pans with the flat of their hands, in the hope of frightening away the hordes of invading insects.

At the age of 18, I wanted a career that would use both my mind and my body in a place where my daily life would involve real commitment, both physical and creative. In farming, every action matters, and every relation with the natural world is a responsible act. The least intervention can have a positive or a negative impact. Running a farm, you are forever making choices; you have to think about your production methods and keep them constantly under review by observing the results. Farmers are in harmony with life when they are able to produce something that is wholesome and attractive to the consumer while respecting the environment. Being a farmer means learning to understand the reactions of the soil, and the life cycle of the fauna and flora, and how to adapt to the climate. This is what living on the land is about.

After a childhood spent remote from this great wealth of experience-based knowledge, I returned to my roots. I went to work with sheep farmers in the Pyrenees. In 1971, I felt myself in sympathy with the peasants of the Larzac who were fighting against the expansion of the military camp. We had in common that link with the soil which had lain dormant in me but been reawakened. At their request, I settled, without title or rights, on a little farm that had recently been appropriated by the Army as part of its programme of land seizures. I was a squatter against military might; it was an unequal contest.

This return to my origins made me think about the importance of roots. Even those who have lived in the city for generations remember where they originally came from. The persistence of this attachment is revealing even if it is an inadequate basis for a re-engagement with rural life. To re-immerse oneself is not to make a nostalgic return to a past that is long gone; it is to seek out what is the basis of any enduring construction. Immersion in rural life brings increased awareness of this profound reality.

The Larzac was a platform for a return to the land, a laboratory for the reconstruction of local and regional agriculture, diversified and adapted to the natural environment.

François Dufour's first memories are of the family farm in Manche, in Normandy. As he worked in the fields, he could see Mont Saint-Michel, symbol of endurance and resistance to storms and invasions, a citadel that has remained an island. François has experience of every type of agriculture now around – traditional, self-sufficient, village, intensive, market-driven and organic. Here, on the same family farm, he has lived through all the transformations of farming life, the move to industrialization, the race for productivity, and then a reconversion to mixed farming, and a return to his roots. Like José Bové, he remembers the peasant farming of the past.

When I summon up my earliest memories of peasant life, they are of working horses, milking cows, suckler cows with their calves, and fields of fodder crops to feed the livestock. I can still see in my mind's eye the corn harvest and threshing in the farmyard. Above all, as a child, I was caught up in the rhythm of work performed in common; I was part of a unity of life, and I learned to share in the solidarity and communal spirit of a village.

The neighbouring farms were of the same type as that of my parents, small or medium-sized, with four or five men working the fields. In winter, men went from one farm to another, cleaning out the cowsheds every fortnight, removing the manure and building dung heaps in the fields for compost.

Muck-spreading, woodcutting and hedging were teamwork, and the men always turned up on time. The farmers were not rivals, subject to market pressures; mutual aid came first, even before selling their produce. The very smallest farms employed a single man full-time or as a day-labourer.

My father and the neighbours re-hooped the barrels using thin rods of chestnut and willow ties. In winter, when the snow made it impossible to go out to the fields, we opened up the rope workshop. In an old building, the men gathered round a fireplace and started up the binding machine. A drill was mounted on a frame of planks equipped with a cone with four grooves and hooks to attach the threads. The job needed four men, who worked as a team. One rolled the recovered or bought threads into a ball, another hooked them on, and a third turned the handle of the drill, leaning on the machine. Under the weight of the man who turned, the threads inserted into the grooves of the cone were twisted together. A fourth man, sitting on a chair, knotted the end of the rope. My father passed the end through the flames. These ropes had many uses: tying up animals, or binding bales of hay, boots and faggots.

When the apple harvest came round, the last dregs of cider were emptied out of the barrels; they were then washed out in hot water to which sulphur had been added to get rid of the acid smell. The left-over cider was made into vinegar. This home-made vinegar was used for salads, but it was also the ingredient in a cure. When an animal had something wrong with one of its limbs – for example, if a horse had a problem in a joint – my father took some good clay from the ground, made a bandage from a strip of canvas sacking, moistened it with the vinegar, and applied it to the fetlock of the affected limb. When a newborn calf had diarrhoea, we didn't call the vet; instead, we put some hay into a bucket of boiling water, left it to infuse, and then fed this 'hay tea' to the calf. Three or four days after drinking it, the calf began of its own accord to suckle its mother again.

Once we had got caught up in the cycle of productivity at all costs, we began to leave it to the factories to process our farm produce, and all our knowledge and skills were lost. The real break came in the years 1968–70, with the appearance of the first bulldozers on the larger farms. I myself, when I took over the family farm, embarked on the intensive production of fodder crops and maize. I abandoned this system in 1985.

2   How the Citizen
Sees Farming

At the dawn of the third millennium, city children of primary school age see things very differently from the grandson of peasants who left and then returned to the land or the son of a long-established peasant farmer. What the children see is factory farming and the packaged, processed foodstuffs arrayed on supermarket shelves. Their view of reality is limited, filtered and distorted, even more so than that of their parents, who themselves came from a generation already cut off from the farming world.

Many little children in city nursery schools have no idea where eggs come from. They have never seen a laying hen. Ask them to draw one, and they don't know how, the nearest they come to them being a pack of white chicken flesh. Douglas Coupland, the American author of *Generation X*, imagines the emergence of an 'ultra-hen' by the year 2080, guaranteed without wings or legs, consisting only of white meat. If you ask schoolchildren old enough to be learning to read what farming is, they will tell you about corn fields and herds of cows, which they have seen only from the windows of a high-speed train. They may mention pigs, though they are never now seen in the open, except in the Corsican scrub, when they get confused with wild boar. Their description of agriculture is confined to the two activities that are most visible today, cereal production and cattle farming.

To them, milk is a drink of unknown origin which comes in cartons or plastic bottles. It is the same colour as its containers, lined up on the supermarket shelf. It is true that the odd school class gets taken to visit a dairy farm and peers through a glass panel at an automated process they only vaguely understand. Children have no idea that a cow can produce milk only if it has calved. Only those lucky enough to go on cottage holidays with their parents have this explained to them, or have the opportunity to stroke a newborn calf. Who thinks of teaching the process by which a mother's milk rises to generations who have not themselves been breast-fed? City-dwellers may escape into the country at every possible opportunity, but they do not see sheep farming, poultry farming, fruit growing, horticulture, aquaculture, fish farming (though the relevant ministry is called 'of Agriculture and Fisheries'), viticulture or silviculture as part of agriculture. They have a worse than reductive vision of it that includes only the most industrialized sector. These are the blinkers the education system puts on our children in the guise of spectacles. And the media are as guilty as the adults. But the sphere of agriculture extends to the whole of our environment, land and water; it includes forests, lakes, rivers, seashores, vineyards, orchards and market gardens (including the *hortillonnage* of the marshes of Picardy, which made the news at the time of the dramatic floods in the Baie de Somme in 2001), and also the hill pastures of sheep farming and cheese dairies; nor should we forget oyster beds and mussel farms. If our young citizens are so blinkered when looking at agriculture in general, how much do they know about farmers?

Let us ask their elders. A survey by IFOP (the French Institute for Opinion Polls) carried out in 2000 gives some idea of the tendentious image of the farmer today in the minds of a supposedly representative sample of the general public. The contemporary farmer, we are told, is 'brave, modern and productive'. That is the good news; the bad is that farmers are also 'egotistical and violent'. Do the good qualities outweigh the bad?

Courage is the recurring virtue, as history relates. True courage consists of getting up at three o'clock in the morning. This word, which is ascribed to Napoleon, applies to all those who have had to cope with the emergencies caused by weather and plagues: courage in adversity, ruin and debt. How many of them have lived through wars, natural catastrophes and epidemics, ready to face any trial and pick themselves up again when the dark years have passed? On the farms, women replaced the sons who left for the front in 1914. The peasantry paid an even heavier blood tax than the townspeople. You only have to look at the lists of names on the war memorials of even the tiniest villages in France. In 1865, wine-growers mobilized against phylloxera. In 2000 and 2001, livestock farmers facing the risk of epidemic protested against the spurious solution of slaughtering herds to control the infection. But they fought *for* a true policy of prevention. Their sense of civic duty, in extreme circumstances, no more failed them than their sense of mission in providing food in normal times.

Their adaptability is equally exemplary. They have adapted to natural hazards, adapted to new technology, and adapted to changes in society, productivity, trade unionism and political directives.

But these two qualities have their downside. When the adaptability consists of obeying all orders, even when they are contradictory, and of not objecting to the perverse consequences of an official system, it is blind. And how many directives have been issued! 'Grow Golden Delicious apples', 'Plant sunflowers', 'Concentrate on pigs', 'Switch to battery farming', 'Treat exhausted soils with fertilizer and pesticides', 'Factory farming is the future'. In the 1960s farmers were told that agriculture had to become entrepreneurial. So it did. Tomorrow, it will be regional. No debate. It would be simpler if it was no more than a branch of industry. There are willing volunteers, ever ready for the signal for off. In the past, they did labour services, now they will adapt to anything. At this point, the quality becomes a failing. In the same way, courage can tip over into suicidal behaviour. You can die courageously on the battlefield of technology.

Are our small farmers prepared to dig their own graves, teeth gritted, without complaining, just as long as their bravery is recognized? Courage today would be to say no to a programmed death, and no to a policy that, on the pretext of modernity, is actually regressive and makes farmer into scapegoats.

Wars have taught us that not every order should necessarily be obeyed. The farmers of today are as adaptable and as brave as their ancestors, but the time has now come for them to practise these virtues in their capacity as responsible citizens. If not, they lay themselves open to accusations of violence in the tradition of the *jacqueries*, of relapsing into the corporate egoism and individualism of the polluter, and of seeking to expand their own farms at the expense of others.

It is not the job of farmers to wage social war. Their mission, on the contrary, is one of peace. If, after the Liberation, the farmers had not buckled down to work, France would not have been so quick to forget rationing or to recover its food self-sufficiency. Their sowing and their reaping gave a bruised and humiliated country the feeling that life was starting anew. When the people polled by the IFOP accuse farmers of violence, we should ask where the real violence lies. Faced with the economic violence imposed by the monopoly of the market, the diktats of the decision-makers, and the Hobson's choice offered by the multinationals whose strategy is to commercialize life, their symbolic actions were a last resort. Without a public and festive opposition, civil society was in grave danger of being anaesthetized and cheated.

3 But Where are the Peasant Farmers?

Who are the new farmers who are saying no? And why are they reclaiming the title of 'peasants'?

In the 1960s the word 'peasant' was consigned to the scrap-heap as expressing the very opposite of modernity. It was relegated to the lowest levels of the glossary of pejorative words, along with 'yokel' and 'bumpkin', buried in the communal grave of churls, villeins and serfs. The dogma of productivity prevailed, although production for its own sake is not the prime purpose of agriculture. Wealth creation is a rather more complex phenomenon, situated somewhere between humanitarianism and humanism. The word 'farmer' was more acceptable, and it replaced 'peasant' during the 'Glorious Years' when productivity was king, because it had connotations closer to the industrial norm.

Today, the word 'peasant' has been rehabilitated, and its connotations are positive. It no longer suggests the country bumpkin but the man who is down to earth, who has his feet on the ground. The historian Pierre Miqel has observed that the word 'peasant' is in danger of being salvaged as a badge of quality. Let it reverberate as a heroic epithet, by all means, but let it not be taken over and turned into a hypermarket logo! To reintegrate peasant roots into agriculture is, over and above trade union battles, to testify to the resurgence of the values of the future, because they protect a heritage and its transmissibility to future generations.

Politics hijacks vocabulary. It is forever appealing to the good citizenship and civic responsibility of its constituents. We might talk of a 'plural' agriculture, in opposition to overspecialized intensive agriculture, except that the adjective has too much of an electioneering ring. And ecology has appropriated 'diversity'. Farming, in returning to its peasant roots, respects both biological diversity and a plurality of methods, without falling into the trap of the words misappropriated by the lobbies.

In the countryside, the gulf between rich and poor is increasing. What do the cereal growers of the Île de France and the pig producers of Brittany have in common with the cultivators of central France who practise mixed farming on 10 or 20 hectares of land? There is a social rift between large and small farmers.

The modern 'peasant' is a producer who remains faithful to the origins of agriculture and pays heed to fundamentals. The first function of farming is to produce food. To feed is to give birth and to give life. To make grain grow, to reproduce and to endure are the three essential aspects of the farmer's task. The productivism that now prevails makes an agribusiness of this food-producing role, which it appropriates while confining it to off-soil techniques; it disconnects agriculture from its fundamental base, it shatters the perennial equilibrium between the land, the water in the soil, and the micro-climate, and it deflects men and women from the proper use of natural resources by preventing them from remaining at the junction of elementary exchanges. The second function of farming is to respect the value of what it transmits and puts on the market and to instil a sense of civic responsibility into all the intermediaries in the food chain, so that it is at no point unworthy of its origins. Farming and the food trades will get along together as long as people prefer to consume living products. All that industry puts into circulation are products that are dead.

The farmer finds his true identity in his attachment to the land. But this rootedness is more than just a sense of place, an ancestral heritage, a habit and a way of life. It deserves to be perpetuated not as a right of ownership but because it is based on a labour that is creative of wealth. To be unable to make a living, despite devoting one's life to this production of added value, advantageous to all categories of the population, is an economic iniquity and a social disorder.

When farmers are compensated for the slaughter of their herds after an outbreak of foot-and-mouth disease, they get all or part of the market value of the animals that are destroyed, but no one considers their psychological trauma. The suspicion and the doubt cast on the quality of their work are difficult for them to bear.

A few years after the end of the Second World War, one in four of the French population worked on the land. The Farmers Statute of 1946 represented a social advance. There were then between 7 and 8 million active peasant farmers. By 1990, their number had fallen to 1,500,000, on fewer than a million farms, and by 2001 to only 664,000. In Brittany alone, there has been a reduction of 44 per cent in ten years.

According to the experts, if the trend continues at this rate, there will be about 500,000 farms in 2005.

As the number of farms has shrunk, so they have increased in size; the average area is now 45 hectares. The cereal-growers subsidized by a bonus per hectare are taking over unclaimed land; 1 per cent of farmers have more than 200 hectares, and 10 per cent account for 66 per cent of total income. These are the agro-managers.

As they are becoming fewer, farmers are getting younger; the average age has fallen to 38. At the last census, in 1999, the farming sector accounted for 4.5 per cent of the work force. In 2001, it had fallen to below 4 per cent.

Overall, their standard of living is higher than that of those forced to leave the land for the towns, but the gulf between the living standard of the agro-managers and that of the small farmers is wide and getting wider. This great social divide is too easily forgotten.

For many young people, as they see their parents abandoning the struggle in the face of the decline of small farms, the steadily rising toll of losses is evidence of an irreversible phenomenon. At least this is what is said in financial circles. But the decline of high-quality agriculture is not inevitable.

There is a certain, largely regional, literary genre that helps to reinforce a backward-looking, archaic image of the peasant farmer through its regretful and nostalgic evocation of a world that is past. Its authors are well-intentioned; they seek to preserve and transmit a memory and make their readers appreciate local figures, people of character, rebels. But the city-dwellers who read their work are left feeling that the clock cannot be turned back, and that it is all now simply folklore. The very titles, from *La Terre qui meurt* to *Adieu coquelicots*, resound like requiems. Their urban readers are inspired to take their children to discover this ancient history in a museum of popular art and traditions.

The fact that small farmers are disappearing does nothing to stop the farming crisis from continuing to be central to the social debate. It is not impossible for the decline of small farms to be halted, just as unemployment in industry and the service sector has been reduced, despite all the claims that the trend could not be stopped.

Agriculture will remain, in spite of everything, at the heart of society. It is not kept there by political will but by the needs and expectations of civil society.

Food is a constant preoccupation of all peoples, and no society is exempt from the three rules of sufficiency, edibility and preference.

Food can only respond to these three requirements by remaining diversified. Do we want to end up consuming nutritious pills and creams manufactured by agro-industry and distributed from some sort of new sterilized market halls, like terminals in the centres of mega-cities?

Instead of impassively noting that 95 per cent of poultry and pigs no longer come from real farms – the same proportion as for cereals – and instead of seeing the few eccentrics who go on making high-quality products in remote corners of France as a species doomed to extinction, citizens can revolt and demand food that is natural and that tastes good. An effort of will on the part of society, a demand for quality, and social concerns, can still reverse the trend. There remain, happily, little islands where men and women still cling to identified products with high added value. They have resisted the pressures because the morphology of the land has prevented the bulldozers from being brought in and flattening everything in their path; also, because they believe that the day will come when more and more townspeople will appreciate them. They have not abandoned their prime task, these men and women who remain rooted in, or have returned to, the land.

A visit to Norway gives François Dufour food for thought.

When I went to Norway in February 1982, I was very surprised to observe the cultural level of Norwegian farmers, who spent at least three hours a day reading in their libraries. Every house had a living room with scores or even hundreds of books. I was deeply impressed, and it made me think. The time in which these people were 'cultivating' themselves in their homes was time not devoted to cultivating their land, but this time spent reading and thinking helped to enrich peasant families. The rural world in France has impoverished and alienated itself by supplying primary agricultural produce at low prices to industry. Our farmers have lost all sense of responsibility; they have gradually ceased to behave like people with the capacity to change things, preferring to behave like victims of the system. There is nothing worse than seeing yourself as a victim. The CAP encourages this noxious desire. When subsidies are doled out to compensate for falling prices, the recipients are turned into 'welfare dependents'; they are psychologically and culturally impoverished. When you become a producer of raw materials for industry, or when you make hundreds and thousands of tons of meat a year, you lose a large part of your identity and you lose your ability to think, reflect and act. Productivist agriculture has destroyed both hearts and minds.

Over the last three decades, a number of peasant traditions have been swept away. When farmers stopped threshing their corn in the farmyard and began to rely on the combine harvester, neighbours no longer joined forces to bring in the harvest. This change did away with a century of traditions. Young people, especially the militants of the JAC, had embarked on their farming careers sustained by regular discussion of common problems and educated to accept and apply the farming practices of the green revolution; they came to the end of their careers demoralized and demotivated. The economic pressures and consequent stress of the last twenty years have been so intense that many have left farming worn out and depressed. These 'early-retireds' are best placed to describe their experiences during this period. They have preserved a body of knowledge and skills while paying the price of modernization. Luckily, in a number of regions, there is a desire to transmit an experience that ought not to be lost. If we are incapable of absorbing it and ensuring its survival, what will become of the generations of 2030 or 2050? Nothing will remain of this era of crazy cohabitation between two diametrically opposed types of farming.

Whatever the political developments, there will always be an agriculture. The real danger is that the disappearance of small farms, if it is allowed to continue, will tip the balance and allow farming to fall wholly into the hands of an agro-chemical and agro-industrial system which will, in the end, destroy all diversity; it will force a universal standardization, which is not what people want, especially in France. If this haemorrhaging of farmers is not halted, consumers will be conditioned to accept a homogenous diet.

Townspeople must understand that the battle for quality is their battle, and that it is in their interests not to neglect their duty of solidarity with the minority who provide them with wholesome food. Why should a sector of the population be denied the right to live, especially when it enables the rest of us to live in the manner we choose?

The architecture of the megalopolis conceals from city-dwellers an obvious truth that should never be forgotten: agriculture remains the prime source of human activity. First, in terms of production: it makes it possible to feed the inhabitants of the planet; then in terms of jobs: 60 per cent of humanity lives by agriculture. Yet the decision-makers of today, in their determination to organize farming on the basis of market logic alone, are in the process of radically reducing both our planet's chances of survival and the chances of peoples all over the world to retain the possibility of development. More than a billion peasants in the world today still work their land by hand.

From this perspective, agriculture is the barometer of the condition of the planet, and also its critical mass. If you plan to do away with 80 per cent of the 60 per cent of people who now live in the countryside, and create megalopolises of a hundred million inhabitants, you are initiating a process that will lead to a 'Universe of Concentration Camps', and the displacement, penning up and ghettoizing of whole populations. To seek to apply the logic of the market and the logic of industry to agriculture worldwide is to move towards a world that will be intolerable. What will happen in China, for example, with its more than 800 million peasants, or in India, with 600 million, if it is decided to reduce the number to between 4 and 5 per cent, as in France, or 1 per cent, as in the United States and Great Britain? The result will be 'urban cancers', the proliferation of towns of 100 million or 150 million inhabitants. The balance in terms of environmental survival and resources will be radically altered. In the end, a world will be created that has no future. I believe that people are at last beginning to realize that the problems of the planet cannot be resolved without a clear vision of the future of farming and of the necessity of keeping populations where they now live.

When the Third Republic was created, the voice of the peasantry carried huge weight. The Republic was built on its rural foundations. But with the end of clear majorities, the Republic became less concerned for its peasants. Gambetta had extolled the virtues of a Republic based on its living peasant resources. Today, the Republic has abandoned them.

It is as if the development model that was chosen and the type of industrial society constructed were based on the *elimination of the peasant farmer*. It is not the first time that the peasantry has been cheated. The Republic has experienced a sort of historical perversion. The Revolution began, after all, in the countryside. There would never have been the Estates General without it or without the *cahiers de doléance*. Rural society overwhelmingly demanded change. The Revolution was hijacked, and it was the peasants who lost out. One cannot make sense of the uprisings in the Vendée or the Chouans in general without understanding that the revolt happened because the Revolution had been confiscated by the well-heeled to the detriment of the peasantry. The whole of the west of France rebelled, when they said to themselves: 'No, hang on, you are taking us for suckers! Already, the land has been bought up by people who had money, the new aristocrats; now we are being asked to go and defend the frontiers of this Revolution, which has been turned against us, when it was we who were the first who wanted things changed.' A century later, the same situation recurred: the peasants were used by Thiers to destroy the progressive elements, conscripted by the immutable order, made, in spite of themselves, a bulwark against those who wanted change. In 1870 the peasants were used to destroy the Paris Commune and other insurrectionary movements, for example in Marseille. After this inversion of progressive values, the Republic long maintained the image of the traditions of the countryside and of the peasantry as repositories of eternal values, but completely instrumentalized. Above all, they must not be allowed to move, but must stay put and pay a higher blood tax than the rest of the population. It is astonishing, given the massacre of the thousands killed in the 1914–18 war, that there was not more rebellion in the trenches against this unspeakable butchery. How could villagers not rebel when they read for the fiftieth time the name of yet another dead conscript, or when, for the fiftieth time, the police knocked on a door with the letter that said: 'Your son has died in battle'? The level of submissiveness that prevailed beggars belief. The national order of Pétain exploited the eternal values, the arable and the pastures, the life-blood of France.

Today, the Fifth Republic has attained the ultimate refinement of perversion by associating farmers in their own destruction. 'Joint management', through their majority trade union, with the Ministry of Agriculture consists, behind the kindly mask of hypocritical protection, of lavish, comprehensive aid, of profound regrets on the one hand and congratulations on the other, of asking small farmers to agree uncomplainingly to dig their own graves and destroy their own farms.

When angry voices are heard or justice is demanded, the Jacobins go looking for a strong man with a firm handshake and give him the Agriculture portfolio with the implicit mandate: 'Whatever you do, get them to shut up!' It is true that there have been some uniquely corporatist demonstrations. The present divisions in the farming world are not simply between trade unions: the conservatives accuse the rebels of being reluctant to change, while they themselves wreak havoc in the name of progress by their acceptance of productivity as king.

An unprecedented shift came in the 1970s, with a challenge to productivism. The peasant movement, at least that part of it represented by the Confédération Paysanne and also by other groups, brought farmers back into the social mainstream, and not as a separate category. This movement is based on one fundamental premiss, that there can be no solution for farmers without solutions for society as a whole. If farming is to be revitalized, the peasant movement cannot remain apart from general social developments. Some have criticized our support for causes external to the French rural world, but this is because they fail to realize that there can be no solutions for farmers or for the countryside in general without a wider consideration of social problems. If townspeople, including those living in the inner cities, do not become aware of the need for change in the countryside, it will never happen. The rally of 30 June at Millau seemed to prove the contrary: the 100,000 people who arrived to demonstrate their solidarity with the defendants in the McDonald's trial included many from the towns and in particular from the inner cities, second-generation immigrants among them. The presence of the rock star Zebda was significant; by his declaration that 'you speak to individuals and not to masses' he was saying that we are speaking to the young people in city housing developments as much as to farmers. What is important is that people recognize that the struggle of the farmers is their struggle too. This is the crucial message: every citizen can understand the key issues in this battle, even if they inhabit what appears to be a totally different reality.

This is a revolutionary movement, not in the usual sense of armed insurrection, but in that of a revolution that takes place within the individual and puts him or her back at the centre of history. Individuals are once again agents in their own history. The change does not come from above; it happens in all the routine activities of everyday life, both individual and collective. The methods used to achieve change have to be appropriate to the identified aims, which is why we speak of active non-violence. Non-violence is compatibility between the means and the ends. A just society cannot be created by unjust methods. If you destroy your opponent, you have no one with whom to negotiate later on, and you lapse into dictatorship. If the aim is personal development and respect for rights and democracy, the methods employed at every level must always be in conformity with the desired objectives. We admire the formulation of Gandhi: 'the end is in the means just as the fruit is in the seed'. Every individual is a carrier of the collective message.

A debate about the future of agriculture leads on to many other debates, about training, education, the sort of society we want to live in, personal development or alienation, and the loss, or recovery, of control over the factors that determine an individual's fate. If they can only steer clear of a corporatist approach and keep an open mind, farmers have the capacity to pose the truly important questions.

4 The Spiral of the 'Glorious Years'

When and how, after so many social victories and with such mastery over the elements, did we reach a situation where agriculture has been 'denatured', farmers have been marginalized and then excluded from society, and industrial products have replaced locally produced food? How has it come about that instead of enjoying the pleasures of the table, we feel afraid as we eat ready-prepared foods? How have we managed to transform an art of living – incomparable in France – into a gigantic lottery in which our health is at stake? The change came during what are in France called the 'Trente Glorieuses', the decades between 1945 and 1975.

They were 'Glorious Years' without much glory, to judge by the consequences. During this thirty – or forty – year period, farming adapted to the need to achieve food self-sufficiency. Once the period of growth had ended, or at least stabilized, everything changed. The time had come for the government to adopt a different strategy, to make the point that, quantitatively, a sufficient level of production had been achieved; that what was needed now was to maintain quality; that if no thought was given to the purpose of the job of farming, growth would continue at the expense of the peasants, who had surely earned the right to exist; that there was no bottomless pit of public money, and that markets were not infinitely elastic. What was to be done? Such questions were never posed. The small farmers were dispossessed; they no longer have the power to control their own lives, and the government no longer has the power to make decisions.

When, for example, over time, the production of milk began to be organized – that is, when the farmers who had once produced their own milk, made their own cream and butter, and marketed them locally, began to supply their primary produce to be processed by the dairy industry – the farmers lost much of their power. The idea of organizing and delegating was fine to begin with: if they wanted to do a good job, the argument ran, they would concentrate on production and leave others to do the rest. The problem created by this delegation is that the farmers lost control. We can see the same process of dis-possession and alienation in the case of cereal farming. When farmers were told to go on increasing their yields per hectare and not to worry when their arable soils became increasingly barren ('Don't worry, the chemical industry is perfectly capable of treating exhausted land'), power gradually passed into the hands of a capitalist system, which has looked after its profits but given no thought to the job of the farmer or the utility of his calling. Production was all that mattered, every-thing else was brushed aside, and the powers that be encouraged the process by distributing financial manna with a lavish hand.

The destruction of the countryside and the disastrous redistribu-tion of land have been achieved with the assistance of money injected by governments – the money, that is, of the citizen and the taxpayer. The farmers lost their power as soon as they entrusted the processing of their products to the system and became suppliers to industry. Industry was in a good position to impose a bogus competitiveness on governments in order to increase volumes and yields, getting society as a whole to bear the cost. The state was brought face to face with the 'market': 'You have opted for food self-sufficiency', they were told, 'we are ready to go, the mechanics are all in place; on the one hand, we'll look after the peasants, who will supply us with the raw materials, on the other, we have all the equipment needed for processing and distribution. You are the decision-makers, help us to press even further ahead.'

We are critical of the FNSEA, for being so hungry for power that they have committed farming to joint management with successive gov-ernments. 'We know best, we will decide'; from this point on, the small farmer has been no more than the foot soldier who is despatched to the front. The FNSEA bears its share of responsibility for the negative, or at the very least distorted, image of farmers held by townspeople. The ministers of agriculture and the commissioners in Brussels have relied on the fact that the FNSEA is the majority trade union. As if intent on suicide, the farmers gave a mandate to a few 'apparatchiks'. These are men who have become increasingly detached from their farms and who long ago lost their peasant roots. They still own a farm, and visit it at weekends, but it is many years since they had to deal with the economic and social realities of production, as their main income derives from the exercise of their many responsibilities. These new *seigneurs* no longer look back. They sit comfortably in their armchairs; it is a long time since they got mud on their boots, and gradually, close to power, they have lost sight of the very basis of the role and the mission of agriculture.

Those who bear most responsibility for the crisis are those who refuse to countenance any talk of controls – that is, of adapting supply to demand – and those who refuse to question the model. They are often the decision-makers in the economic sector. You only have to look at the sort of octopus that the FNSEA has become. The board members and the vice-presidents are simultaneously involved at the local level in running the associations of producers, the co-operatives, the Credit Agricole bank, the MSA and Groupama; the same bigwigs manage the real estate within the SAFER. They have a finger in every pie, and it is often they who support the policy at national level, even influence it in their own interests. When it is they who have provoked the crisis, they incite the mass of small farmers to anger and violence. From their own sheltered position, they send out their foot soldiers, who have no more to lose, and they even supply them with their slogans: 'No one listens to us; all the decisions come from the top of politics; the policies are incoherent and do nothing to help us.' Those who suffer the most from this nasty situation are often people who do not join the demonstrations. They take the law into their own hands, in a sense, by leaving farming one way or another – there are numerous suicides. Levels of depression are high, and hospitalizations for breakdowns are common. The farmer returns home after a week of treatment, goes back to work, and then has to be readmitted to hospital. Many farmers are on medication for a large part of their lives and can see no way out of their situation. They end up by admitting defeat, with their debts as their only reward.

The Confédération Paysanne has always rejected the sort of street violence that consists of smashing public buildings, spraying liquid manure, or burning tyres. It is not in its philosophy. It has struggled to achieve a reconciliation with townspeople, and we are sorry when they choose not to recognize this or pretend not to know who is perpetuating the crisis, who jointly manages farming, or who inspires the extremist groups. Those who want to beat up a minister for the environment are always those who have been at the controls for forty years, and who have also been manipulating the politicians. That is the paradox, and the citizen should be aware of this double-dealing.

It is even in the interests of these *agents provocateurs*, who bank on the despair of small farmers, for the demonstrations to get out of hand

and for the damage to be blamed on the little people they want to discredit. They employ them as foot soldiers so that they can more easily be got rid of. The actions are only violent when the situation is already almost lost for the small producers. Those who have provoked the crisis, who manipulate the small farmers and get them to take to the streets in the hope of 'emerging from the crisis', believe that production should go on being increased. The markets may then open up and cause prices to collapse. The people within the system who make these decisions know exactly what they are doing. Sadly, the great mass of small farmers, 95 per cent of the total, does not; they are caught up in the system without realizing it. We believe it is responsible and useful to identify the true culprits in this situation and to ensure, once and for all, that public opinion condemns them. The common error, when these outbursts occur, is to lump all farmers together.

The Confédération Paysanne has engaged in an ongoing dialogue with citizens in the hope of creating a different sort of agriculture; it has chosen to attack the evil by denouncing the process and by advocating reconciliation, mutual understanding, and support for the installation of new 'peasant' farmers and an agriculture that will respond to what it is that the majority of people want: to know what they are putting on their plates. We want to make a new start on a radically different basis, but this cannot be done without the farmers, and it is difficult to get the message across when they are for the most part slaving away, noses to the grindstone. When they are bogged down, it is not the ideal time to try to persuade them to make a change of direction. The mass of small farmers bow to events when what they ought to be doing is making the time to think about how the system can be changed. This is a hard task, since, when things are not actually getting worse, people tend to discover that they are, after all, OK as they are.

François Dufour broke with this system in 1985. What happened to make him say no to productivist agriculture?

How could I work all through the 1970s with people who had lost all connection with living things? At the time, the apologists for the system were very persuasive in their dealings with young people. We were to be part of a great modernizing adventure; we would be working in less arduous conditions, increasing our incomes, living well off the fruits of growth, enlarging our parents' farms, and so on. We embarked on a course of action that was completely crazy. In order to increase our production of fodder crops, we began to grow maize.

After five or six years of this monoculture the land is exhausted; the humus content of the soil is depleted, it deteriorates and becomes inert. It has to be treated by stepping up the applications of fertilizer. This palliative chemical treatment is onerous. Far from diminishing, difficulties multiply; imbalances appear both in the harvests and among the livestock, and the treatments destabilize the farm budget.

When an animal's feed is unbalanced, it needs more frequent veterinary interventions, and more products have to be used, as it has to be given minerals and vitamins. The greater the imbalance in the diet, the greater the need to reintroduce primary materials or sophisticated products.

The schedule does not allow for the fact that the least vagary of the climate can hold operations up. The system required us to sow maize on an impoverished soil between 15 and 30 April. A couple of windy days means that a crust forms on the soil and the maize will not grow through. If it does, and there is a cold snap in June, the maize is chilled and turns violet. It has to be given a nitrogenous boost. The yields fall, and the costs of production rise because of the need to treat the chilled maize. The problems of this mode of production are obvious, but you only learn by experience. Brussels takes no notice.

Between October and April, between two crops of maize, an Italian ray grass, a cattle food, is grown at top speed. It is sown in the autumn, when the sap is falling. Constant applications of fertilizer are required. The crop is harvested very early, on 15 April, so that the ground can immediately be sown with maize. It is ensiled overnight, and the ploughing, muck-spreading and sowing is done next day. You have to work flat out.

The more land is ploughed in the spring to grow maize and yet more maize, the less land is left for growing grass for the animals.

In July, if there is a dry spell, the supply of grass runs out; you have to raid the silos where the fodder crops are stored under tarpaulin, although the silage is meant for the following winter.

The constant ploughing of the soil, the costs of ensiling, storage, fertilizers, nitrogenous correctives, legumes, animal feed and the capital investment mean that the farmer is walking a tightrope. When you come to do your sums, you realize that the surplus has already been earmarked, for industry or the bank.

We discussed it as a family and decided that we could no longer go on in the same way. The system meant we were achieving a higher turnover in return for a smaller income. And with all the ingredients that were bought in from outside, we felt as if we were busy servicing a dead agriculture rather than a living one. This discussion was a turning point. Something was badly wrong; we had to rethink our fodder systems, our relation to the soil, and our working conditions, our life-style, and our relations with the consumer. If you go on using ever more products from outside to maintain yields, it is possible (we were not yet certain, but were eventually proved right) that you are degrading the food you produce. What sort of agriculture is this? At this point, we said: 'At the end of the day, if we look back over the last five, eight or ten years, it is true that we have increased our turnover, but we have been working for an industry that dominates us, imposes a technology on us, and is driving us mad.' We discussed matters with other militants and came to the conclusion that it was time to stop; we had to extricate ourselves from this vicious circle.

We were not alone in coming to this decision. All around us, farmers had converted to more natural methods. Many others were anxious to escape from the system. Why did they not do so as quickly as they wanted? Because they had been trapped into an investment programme. When they had opted for a productivist and intensive agriculture, they had often made a clean sweep of the techniques and practices they had previously employed in buildings that were unsuited to factory or off-soil farming.

When you go to a bank with a specific project in mind, you often come away with a project on a much grander scale. If you want to set up a small workshop or buy a medium-sized tractor, the lender will not finance you; you are too small, not profitable enough. You have to think big, you have to join an association of producers or be integrated into one of the big production chains. You are then caught up in a cycle; you are locked into the system, and the situation is turned on its head. Once you have begun to work within the new system, you have to make a profit and technical advances in order to pay off your loan before even thinking about an income for yourself. Farmers have been transformed by having technical choices forced on them that cut them off from their relations with agriculture and nature. The best way for big business to control farmers is to keep them permanently in debt. Once you have to answer to somebody else every morning, when the minute you wake up you say to yourself: 'Today I have to give so much to the bank, so much to this firm, and so much to that organization', you have become part of the productivity cycle, but without benefit to your income or your family; the only beneficiary is the system that you continue to enrich. You are a prisoner of crises over which you have no control: crises of overproduction, where the instability of the market, which has been organized, causes prices to fall and you face a bumpy ride; health crises, too, because intensive large-scale livestock farming involves an enormous concentration of animals in one place. The more the animals are confined, the more debilitated they become, and the enterprise is in a permanent state of turbulence. The system has been well thought out at the two ends of the chain; it has been devised so that whenever there is a health problem, you call on a package of technical assistance to solve it. You fight a losing battle for income and a losing battle for profits, and you no longer have time to think. Finally, the day arrives when you reach such a pitch of weariness that, like so many other farmers as they approach 50, you say 'I can't wait to escape from this vicious circle!'

There are many farmers who recognize the predicament they are in, but once they are caught up in the system, it is difficult to escape. If you are a pig or poultry producer for one of the big factory farming chains, for example, you cannot extricate yourself from the system from one day to the next. If, on the other hand, you maintain your links with the soil – that is, put your animals out to pasture – you are able to change your practices much more easily because you are still free to make your own decisions. But to get back to this situation, you have to recover control of all the parameters. Until recently no organizations existed to help farmers change direction. Everything was arranged to make it easy to start working within the dominant system, but if you decided to adopt a different approach, rediscover a meaning to life, and escape a situation that condemned you to perpetual failure, you were on your own, in a total desert. The best you could hope for was to meet a few like-minded oddballs, and resolve to return to the old habit of exchanging ideas and information; you might establish a tight-knit group, where there could be an open and tolerant debate, and where everybody spoke the same language so that they could understand and try to support each other. To do this you had to make contact with people from outside the dominant circles, who could help you to make your escape.

As the majority of farmers are heavily in debt, they have to change direction slowly, think carefully about what they are doing, be aware of all the parameters, and aim for maximum autonomy: autonomy in decision making; autonomy in relation to the finance companies so that you can try gradually to get out of debt; and autonomy at the level of the marketing circuits that lack any respect for the farmer's work. Are city-dwellers aware that for forty years now small farmers have no longer made out their own bills? When they provide a product to a firm, it is no longer they who decide the selling price; it is the firm that says what it is willing to pay; it appropriates the parameters that have been decided elsewhere. It takes no account of the farmer's production costs; it rules: 'This is the price you will get today.' Little by little, we farmers have seen it become normal for payment for our produce to be made a month after delivery, even three months in some sectors. To recover our autonomy would be to recover the means to negotiate the selling price of our produce – that is, recover our power. By this I mean the power to revive a relationship with living things and with the consumer, but also with the citizen. There can be no change and no solutions unless we recover control of all the parameters so that we can go back to our roots and get our feet back on the ground.

My family and I managed to make our change of direction over a period of ten years. It was a lengthy process, but it has restored our freedom to think and act.

5 The True Cost of the Common Agricultural Policy

Let us now assess the true cost of a policy costing billions of francs, a profligacy that is played down as far as possible in case a comparison with the cost of organic production proves unfavourable to the CAP, and reveals that it is not actually profitable at all (even though it is based on productivity).

For forty years, fantastic, fabulous sums of money have been doled out; this is the paradox of a grandiose and ruinous agriculture that is still lauded as being 'cheapest' for the consumer.

What is the per capita cost of the subsidies from Brussels?

Every European taxpayer pays the CAP every day of his or her life about 7 francs. Yes, comes the reply, every French citizen pays 7 francs, but French farming receives more from Brussels in economic aid than France contributes to the cost of the CAP; so, overall, for the 7 francs we pay we get 10 francs in return. But who benefits from this income? Not the taxpayer! Another argument is put forward by the commissioners: 'You have to understand what society wants; if people want to have plenty of everything on their plates, they have to pay for it.' If only paying dearly for the CAP meant quality was guaranteed! If only it meant that we had wholesome produce on our tables, and that we were spared the endless health scares that we face these days! In fact, the opposite is the case, and the image of farming has been tarnished. Misery for the farmer has not meant happiness for the consumer.

All through this period, as the concentration of production has continued apace, and as piggeries and poultry houses have grown to gigantic proportions, by dint of ignoring all its negative consequences, it has been claimed that this type of farming is profitable.

The application of industrial logic to food production has meant that more and more was produced so that more and more could be sold, and sold cheap. Its greatest success has been to put a bog-standard chicken on the market at less than 10 francs a kilo, or pork at 7 francs a kilo, even 5 francs in times of crisis; yet the cost to the farmer is 9 francs, if you simply add up the price of the young pig, its food, buildings depreciation, water and electricity, making no allowance for labour costs, the input of the farmer, or all the unpleasant after-effects. For as this standardization has proceeded, society has been left to bear the cost of dealing with the consequences, for example, all the crises in which so many farmers have disappeared. The crises of overproduction designed to bring down prices and adapt, or so it is claimed, to the market, have been organized, willed and orchestrated, consigning many thousands of farming families to the scrap-heap. The farmer who loses his job receives no unemployment benefit, but he has to be redeployed elsewhere. The moral and social prejudice is huge, not only for the bankrupt farmer but also for his family and his children, and for all those who had supported and advised him at various times. It is society that has to take responsibility for him, once he is no longer productive. Nor should we forget the medical costs of treating his overwork, stress and depression.

To persuade us that the CAP promises a brilliant future, the balance of trade in the food industry is frequently painted in glowing colours. When the cost of the raw materials bought to sustain this agriculture is calculated, and compared with the proceeds from sales, the surplus turns out to be very weak. The energy costs ought also to be included – for example, those of the pig and poultry production established in the west of France and certain other parts of Europe. First, there is the energy cost of the transport of raw materials to feed operations that are concentrated into one region. Huge quantities of vegetable feeds are imported; cargoes of soya beans and cassava are constantly crossing the oceans at immense cost. Second, there is the cost of transporting the processed meat, which is sent back across whole countries, even oceans, to be sold and made available to consumers thousands of kilometres away. To get some idea of this monstrous traffic, you need only go to one of the motorway toll stations south of Paris and count the number of lorries registered in Finistère or Côtes-d'Armor that pass through between ten in the evening and three in the morning, night after night after night. The stream of refrigerated lorries loaded with frozen or chilled meat leaving for distant markets is surely the very model of wastefulness.

When you see everything that converges on Brittany, and everything that leaves every night for other regions, you realize that this perpetual motion makes no sense. At that price, this sort of agriculture is far from profitable. Not only does it fail to provide the farmer with an income, or to satisfy the consumer, but it will eventually bring a phenomenal environmental cost. Lastly, not only is the nation's money being squandered on this sort of activity, but this profligacy is also putting future generations into debt. If we continue to impoverish the soils and pollute the water for decades, a day of reckoning will surely come. But whose will be the money used to pay the ecological bill?

In fact, the tax-paying citizen is still discovering the true debit side of the bill: on top of the cost of the subsidies comes the cost of putting right the mistakes. The chemical impact of intensive agriculture looms over our daily life. It is only when there are scares about the level of pesticides or weed-killers such as atrazine in the water that the connection is made. Ecological disasters give a further boost to business. People end up paying for their water three times over: they pay for the public water supply, they pay taxes for cleaning up polluted watercourses, and they buy bottled water because their tap water is undrinkable. They are also taxed through the cost of Social Security payments and the Health Service, because the system makes people ill. For farmers there may even be yet another tax, if they are obliged to install de-nitrification plants on their farms to stop their animals from falling sick after drinking piped or tap water. This is because the public water supply, to which chemicals have been added, is extremely harmful to young animals. Livestock farmers have to bear the cost of purifying their water.

The productivist system pushed to the limit has been a bottomless pit, and now we have to deal with the damage it has inflicted over the decades. Intensive livestock farming predicated on the export, and therefore transport, of animals is more vulnerable to the spread of viruses. It was amply demonstrated in 2000 that agriculture cannot control epidemics and that the drastic measures decided as a matter of urgency, in defiance of good sense and pandering to popular opinion, dangerously increased the agricultural debt. The cost of the systematic slaughter and incineration of whole herds and of the disposal of the remains is currently a major drain on the agricultural budget; the balance remaining at the beginning of the year 2001 has been completely swallowed up.

From this bottomless pit, a tiny part of the budget finds its way to farmers in the form of subsidies. But this aid is a double-edged weapon. It benefits the better-off and hastens the demise of those worst hit by the system. As much as 80 per cent of the subsidies from Brussels goes to 20 per cent of farmers. Under a claim of fairness for all in the application of European regulations, the money is distributed in the least fair way imaginable. The distribution is based on criteria of accessibility. In this case, the criteria are such that a large majority of farmers receive nothing. At the beginning of 2001, the Minister of Agriculture, Jean Glavany, announced 1.4 billion francs in aid; of this sum, 200 million was allocated without consultation to those who had contracted debts, so that their bank charges could be taken care of or their Social Security contributions remitted. Those who are up to date with such payments will get nothing, even if they are struggling to cope with their suppliers' bills, having not unreasonably given priority to covering their contributions. What will happen to the rest of the money? None of it will reach the very poorest.

This iniquity penalizes the majority of small milk-producers in France, farmers with between twenty and thirty-five cows who produce between 100,000 and 150,000 litres of milk. They do not meet the criteria. They live independently on their farms and still decide their own future, but twice a year they have to tighten their belts one more notch. In their case, the sale of meat products – that is, of cull cows – represents at most 10, 12 or 15 per cent of their turnover. To qualify for aid, there has to be what is called a 'specialization level' of 30 per cent in the meat sector, within the total operation. As a result, they receive no compensation. If they sold four cows during the year, at a loss of 2,500 francs per head, they face an overall loss of 10,000 francs, the equivalent of two and a half months of the family income.

When you look back over the last twenty years, the response to every crisis, whether of health, overproduction or markets, has been to apply the same criteria: aid is proportionate to the volume of production. The middling farmers get a little whiff of oxygen to keep them going; the large farmers get the lion's share, a sort of perk of office; the bottom category gets nothing at all. The category in receipt of the most generous support has the means to take over the farms abandoned by those who get none. It is a procedure that encourages the concentration of production and the elimination of peasant farmers. The little men are destroyed, the middle-sized farmers struggle on until the next crisis, and the biggest – with the community's money – offer to solve the problems thus created. We, they point out, were able to adapt (a thank-you to the Minister of the Economy and Finances), and we are ready and able to take over the vacant land and the production capacity of those poor chaps who couldn't hack it. Whereas the truth is that these poor chaps have been spurned by a government that gave them no support. But they are made victims, and blamed, while others, at the other end of the spectrum, sit waiting to absorb them.

In 2001, for the first time, the Minister of Agriculture set ceilings for aid. Were we about to hail a great 'first'? Alas, no, as he omitted to change the system for qualifying. The most vulnerable and the smallest, those who are barely keeping their heads above water, risk sinking even further into misery. The system continues to function as it has done for thirty years. To think that it was built up from nothing in order for every crisis to lead to restructuring! For the technocrats, 'restructuring' means weeding out the 'worst'. Who exactly are these lame ducks? In economic terms, they are those who do not pull their weight. But in relation to what? In relation to an infernal machine. What an upside-down world it is that punishes in this way the very men and women to whom we owe most of our quality products! Living largely autonomously, less dependent on external systems, these farmers often produce their own fodder to feed their animals. It is they who produce the best-quality meat, since they have more control over the process. Their coherent and transparent production presents least risk in terms of health, and it costs society least dear. If they are to be encouraged, there will have to be an assessment of the assistance they need based on a careful investigation carried out in each small region of production.

Dairy farms, too, are hit by the collapse in meat prices. The majority of the cows known as 'cull cows' have had two, three or four calves; their meat has perhaps a greater density than some types of meat, but it is still of good quality. The farmers are the principal victims of the process, since these cows have often been fed high-protein cattle feed, produced with the remains of rendered livestock, to increase their milk production; people are suspicious and avoid minced meat made with the flesh of cull cows. Here, surely, is a case deserving of aid, but, unhappily, crisis follows crisis without any revision of the criteria for qualifying. Farmers hear about subsidies on the radio and the television, but the fact is that, over the last thirty years, in spite of all the crises, between 60 and 70 per cent of them have never qualified for even the smallest benefit; the public, meanwhile, remains convinced that billions have been pumped into agriculture. This has not happened by chance.

The European Union wanted to force farmers to organize into associations of producers (there was no aid if they didn't). It makes sense, in theory, to organize so as to control volumes of production, but the fact is that, over the years, farmers have grown sick of the way the co-operatives have been managed, and of their attempts to force farmers into a single mould. Small farmers have preferred to retain their independence. The result is that they have been excluded from subsidies. The number of people who leave farming every year and are not replaced has been estimated at about 50,000. In return, only about 10,000 young people have set up on farms. With the present system of farming subsidies many others who would like to go into farming cannot do so, because they do not qualify for assistance; everything has been rigged so that there are fewer and fewer people in the circuit. The farming career is too inaccessible to would-be farmers. What other trade is so restricted?

The 40,000 workers lost every year means 40,000 unemployed, or at least 40,000 persons without employment. This is a loss to the nation. If we add together the unemployment benefits, the lost social security contributions, the medical and psychological treatment of unemployed persons who feel excluded, and their non-consumption in the economic system if they lack the essential minimum, the total social cost of the loss of one worker can be reckoned at 250,000 francs a year, a figure that has to be multiplied by 40,000. This is the first negative effect.

The second loss is the cost to the nation of the constant restructuring of agriculture. Take the case of a farm surrendered by the farmer. It has often received subsidies and public assistance, the benefits of which are abandoned to a landowner who then speculates on its property value and sells the buildings and the land to a buyer who simply wants a second home. The farm disappears, and the farmer is deprived of the benefit of all the subsidies handed out over the years.

A third perverse effect is that all these changes in landownership and all this restructuring tempt the neighbouring farmers into the rush to expand. This comes at a considerable cost because, if the farmer meets the criteria for qualifying for aid, he may receive subsidized credit. At every opportunity, such farmers turn to the state and say: 'The farm next to mine is free, I'm going to take it, I want to expand, but it will be difficult to finance, so give me a subsidized loan.' Expansion on these terms consumes considerable funds.

Nor, last but not least, should we forget another loss, that of all the costs that are euphemistically called the 'negative externalities' of the intensification of factory farming, such as the accumulation of chicken droppings or the damage to groundwater. It would be an interesting exercise to add up all the sums of money that Brussels or the French government distribute every year in the regions in the attempt to clean up watercourses or rebuild pumping stations destroyed by the accumulation of nitrates in maize fields that extend right up to the watercourse banks.

We should also include in our audit of the global cost of productivism all the money that is now being distributed in certain areas to re-create strips of grass alongside watercourses where the banks have subsided because hedges have been grubbed up.

This is the financial balance sheet of forty years of this agricultural policy. The system survives only because, on the one hand, the permanent restructuring is heavily subsidized, while, on the other, the task of making good the damage resulting from a general impoverishment is being left to future generations.

The desertification of the countryside, where some areas fall into decay and farms are abandoned, while production is increasingly concentrated in others, creates imbalances and repeated crises. We have already drawn attention to the energy costs of the concentration of almost all poultry and pig farming in the west of France, and of cereal production in the Île de France. Cargoes of nitrogenous proteins are transported across the Atlantic, while meat from the west of France is distributed all over Europe.

Where has all this frenzied activity got us? Where is the economic gain from industrial livestock farming? The only result of this crazy growth has been a fall in meat consumption. If many people have become reluctant vegetarians during the recent beef crisis, this is no bad thing in itself, but it is a disaster for farming.

The worst economic folly is to take advantage of damage to the environment (pollution of the subsoil and groundwater, high heavy-metal content) in order to generate wealth.

We have ended up adopting destruction followed by reconstruction as an industrial practice. We have accepted the logic of the concrete-manufacturers. By 2005, the whole of France will be criss-crossed by autoroutes; what will we do next, destroy those that exist and build new ones? No, we will widen all the roads connecting one small town to another, making them two lanes in each direction. We must build for the sake of building. We might as well put marble pavements on either side of every forest bridle path. It has become 'normal' to keep the wheels of industry turning with pointless projects. The Hague,

which has prospered thanks to its reprocessing plants, has redistrib-
uted large sums of money to numerous little communes; some with
only a few hundred inhabitants got a million francs a year. The local
elected representatives had no idea how to spend the money. So what
did they do? They concreted everything in sight. They built bridge-
heads everywhere, and they cemented the gutters running between
villages. At Osmonville-la-Petite, after a fierce twenty-minute storm,
torrents of water rushed to the bottom of the village and flooded the
houses. A grandmother of 80 tried to climb onto a table to escape the
water and lost her balance. The water rose up to the ceiling, and
she was found dead. Others had fled a few hundred metres away. The
developers didn't think the water would move so quickly. As everything was concreted over, the speed of the flow was increased. They
had forgotten that the old gutters and the long grass helped to check
the flow. This is what happens when you manufacture concrete simply
to keep industry going. The heresy of 'producing in order to produce'
has infected agriculture.

The figures don't add up, and a day of reckoning will surely come.
Our analysis justifies our claim that either the CAP has been deceived
or it has deceived us.

For years now society has paid increasingly less for its foodstuffs
but increasingly more for all the consequences of the processes supposed to make agriculture competitive. Now the citizen has to meet
the cost of all the health crises; we have reached the stage where we
have to pick up the pieces shattered by the previous system. Society
paid to put the system in place; it is now blowing up in its face. In 1998
the European Community paid 500 million euros to the taxpayers of
the Netherlands in order to eliminate swine fever; this was at a time
when mad cow disease was raging and dioxins and other such plagues
were spreading. The management of these epizootics now absorbs a
significant proportion of the European budget. The cost is exorbitant.
It is known, for example, that the bill for the BSE crisis is likely to rise
to about 45 billion francs in the European Union, an enormous sum,
equivalent to two-thirds of the budget that the European Union
returns to France each year. The support now given to livestock
farmers, currently 1.4 billion, which is very far from compensating
them for their loss, pales into insignificance beside the 45 billion
francs swallowed up thanks to the irresponsibility of an industrial
system that aims to globalize this economy. The English animal feed
manufacturers ought to be liable, but it is not they who pay for the
damage. It is the European taxpayer. The first victims are the small

farmers. And, unbelievably, during those crazy years, when England was getting rid of its ground-up cows any way it could, the cattle feed manufacturers bought them cheap and prospered. The food processing industry had never had it so good. It was a period of galloping restructuring; it took the processing industries that invested billions less than five years to make a profit on their investment. All this indecent profit has to be measured by the yardstick of a taxpayer who has paid for a proportion of the damage and a small farmer who has been crushed by the machine. Society is now busy paying the cost of the consequences of productivism, when the money would be better spent financing a different type of agriculture.

When the Elysée praises French agriculture as the best in the world, how are we to interpret and justify this award of first prize?

We get first prize for profitability. Yet the overall balance sheet shows French agriculture to be ruinous, as we have shown. We are the best in the world when it comes to technical achievement. We lead the field in terms of the number of piglets born each year. The productivity per square metre of our poultry industry is second to none. Record yields are produced in some parts of France in terms of cereals per hectare. And at the same time, we excel in the niche market of foodstuffs with high added value, and in the sophisticated treatment of produce of high quality. Praise is due in particular to our viticulture and to certain farm products.

One thing is sure: we are leaders in an agriculture of crisis. We hold the record for social crisis. The more we export to a world market, the more small farmers we lose. Only England can rival us here.

6 From Junk Food to 'Good Food'

In the 1980s the term preferred by the media in any discussion of food prices was the 'housewife's shopping basket'. The supermarkets based their publicity on their low prices. People gradually came to believe that it was now possible to eat well and cheaply at the same time, and the proportion of the family budget devoted to foodstuffs began to decline. In 1960 it was 34 per cent; thirty years later it had fallen to 18 per cent, and by 2000 to 15 per cent. Of this modest, not to say meagre, sum, the French consumer devoted only 4 per cent to farm produce. José Bové denounced what he called 'malbouffe', which can be roughly translated as 'junk food'. The expression has quite eclipsed the famous 'housewife's shopping basket'. It has spread like wildfire throughout the world; there is no more scathing term in the French language. Jöel de Rosnay, scientific director of the Cité de la Villette, coined the word in 1974. Used by Bové, it assumed universal significance. He made it his own in Millau in 1999 at the time of the symbolic dismantling of a McDonald's.

I remember Jöel de Rosnay's book (*La Malbouffe*), a guide to eating well so as to live well. I was taken aback by its unusual form, that of a recipe book. We began to use the word in our discussions with friends about where farming had gone wrong. But it was never used as a slogan before the events in Millau.

I have searched for an earlier use, but without success. It was at Millau that it was first adopted in an attempt to unite the farming world and the urban world in the face of a phenomenon of which they were both victims, as farmer or as consumer. The day of the demonstration against the symbol of McDonald's, I sensed that we could use this particular word to great effect to show what linked the farmer to the consumer and to condemn the disastrous developments on behalf of both. Contrary to the claims of some of our critics, our aim was not to hold peasant farmers up to opprobrium by suggesting it was they who were responsible for junk food. It was rather to show that junk food was a concept that had been introduced by the food processing industry, advertising and the supermarkets in order to standardize both the mode of production and the mode of consumption. It designated what was driving the peasant farmer off the land, removing all purpose from his labour, and at the same time depriving the consumer of cultural diversity; it was a reminder of the natural order and of the link between production and culture.

Taste itself has been conditioned to make the consumer lose the desire for farm and market-garden produce.

Standard tastes have been distorted. I have watched the transition from one mode of consumption to another. I still have very clear memories of the milk carts that once trundled round most towns. I used to go and visit my grandparents in Brussels, a capital city, where the milkman passed by every morning, his cart loaded with bottles; this was in the 1960s, not so very long ago. Even in towns, the milk still came directly from a farm. I remember very clearly the reaction of friends who had never tasted this sort of milk; they didn't like it because it lacked the slight caramel after-taste of UHT or similar milk. In fact, milk was one of the first products whose taste was changed, the 'normal' taste now being that of the sterilized milk in cartons. This is a development of immense significance. A second example is the market success of a smooth puréed potato mix. People now expect their mashed potatoes to taste like the purée 'Mousline'. Children have been brought up on this ersatz confection and think that this is how mashed potato ought to taste. It is no longer made with a particular type of potato, thick, even slightly lumpy, and mixed with butter; it is now a sort of smooth sieved substance made with flakes that have nothing to do with a real potato.

The change in taste dates back to the late 1950s and early 1960s, also the period when we lost the concept of the pleasures of the table, except for a single weekly meal, the Sunday lunch. This shift came about very quickly and has led to a complete change in the way we eat. It was the real moment of separation between town and country. It happened with the generation that left the village to work in the factories at the beginning of the 1960s. These immigrants adapted to another life-style; men and women now both worked outside the home and changed both their buying habits and the way they ate.

In the 1970s the food industry began to use the health factor to gain acceptance for this standardization of taste, in particular through the many 'lite' products. They began to bombard women and families, those who did the shopping, with exhortations to 'think of your figure' and 'count the calories', hence 'low calory food', 'low fat content' and so on. In effect, the idea was to justify colourless, scentless and insipid food on health grounds. They ruthlessly exploited dietary arguments to sell industrial products. This social phenomenon has coincided with the promotion of household brands. At more or less the same time, two key products were put on the market. First, washing powders, more or less standard items, but sold under clearly identified brand names, which began to add some trick or some gadget. The second was yoghurt; it was in the marketing campaign for this product that a brand began for the first time to position itself on the basis of its 'lightness', the famous 'nought per cent fat'. In this logic, the demand leads to constant proliferation, because the brand that ceases to innovate, or to bring out a new product a couple of times a year, is dead in the water. This development has led to the appearance of increasingly artificial products that are effectively made attractive by playing on the health factor, a paradox indeed.

The advantage for the food industry has been to avoid true visibility; it is easy for the buyer to see the percentage of fat content, more difficult, unless you have been taught how, to see the nutritional value and then appreciate the taste. There is a double deception.

There was an obvious contradiction between these allegedly 'lightened' or modified products and the increasingly standardized products such as chicken breasts, where the identification or definition of the taste was of secondary importance. What mattered was to trumpet the lowest possible price. The consumers bought both the standard chicken and low-fat yoghurt, just as they bought boiled ham that no longer bore any resemblance to the real thing. It is bizarre how basic products have become increasingly standardized while branded goods have grown increasingly artificial; the two processes have gone hand in hand. It seems that the majority of customers never noticed, ready to accept, when it comes to a point, basic products that are crap. Yet Jean Ferret had already denounced this apathy in a song of 1960, *Que la montagne est belle* ('and in the evening we go back to our council flats to eat chicken-with-hormones'). It is hard to accept, but people are prepared to stuff themselves with chicken with added hormones; at first they say how awful it is, but gradually they forget what real chicken tastes like. In fact, just as they accept that hens are kept in battery cages, so they accept a standardized industrial product on their plates. The changing culture and the loss of roots are taken for granted.

This conditioning has been made easier to impose by the way in which the retailing giants have exploited eating habits: people find it reassuring always to buy the same product and the same brand.

If you look at all the different parts of the world, the local population almost always eats the vegetables or cereals that are the staples in their area. Every part of the world has its basic foodstuffs. In France it is wheat and potatoes, in South America beans and maize, in the Maghreb hard corn with vegetables and semolina, and in India rice and lentils. The basic foodstuff, whatever form it takes, is an identical cultural fact.

The art of cooking and the ways of adapting these basic materials are part of the diversity and the richness of cultures. In the past, when you went to the butcher, the grocer or the greengrocer, you bought a certain number of basic products that could be made into a wide variety of dishes; you always bought the same things, but you then used whatever you had bought to make very different dishes. From this we have passed, without transition, to standardized methods of buying, of packets off shelves; we buy products that are already prepared, to which nothing more can be done. If you buy standardized yoghurt or a packet of Mousline purée, you get a sort of curdled milk or a version of mashed potato, but all you can do to either of them is what you are told to do on the packet. With the emergence of the frozen ready cooked meal, prepared foods have become standardized, and individual initiative has been banished from the act of making a meal. In fact, the whole business of providing meals has changed, and the creative dimension has been completely excluded by the retailer. And retailing colluded with the food industry, because for a while they were allies and accomplices, and developed, as it were, hand in hand. Today it is the other way round; the concentration of distribution systems – there remain scarcely five retailers in France – means that it is they who impose price levels on the processors. Now they are going in for 'micro-niches' in an attempt to squeeze yet more profit from processing. The urban wage-earners' weekly supermarket shop, the ritual loading of the shopping trolley every Saturday morning, completely changes the way meals are conceived. Yet it is perfectly possible to behave differently, even in towns; there is nothing to prevent anyone from making soup or vegetables or a roast to last several days. All you need to do is put them straight into the refrigerator. The leftovers can be put to good use. More than the sprint to the shops, time spent in the kitchen is seen as time wasted because it is no longer a time of creativity or of shared meals. All the statistics tell us that less time is now spent round a table, and it is growing even less with every passing year. The United States comes top of the list, the time sitting at table being six minutes; in France it is still about twenty minutes, eating as a family. We are witnessing the complete atomization of individuals with the loss of the sense of the dining table as a place for meeting and socializing. The refrigerator has become the most important piece of furniture; it is where everyone goes to get something to eat, food bought already prepared. It is then eaten standing up, alone, or crossing paths with others who are similarly 'grazing', while watching a virtual relationship on the television.

To be aware that there is another way of conceiving food is in itself an act of resistance and a step towards assuming one's identity. It is also a cultural act and an educational act in relation to the generations, children and the family. You can make a difference by the way you buy. This was amply demonstrated during the mad cow disease crisis, when people spontaneously stopped buying meat, possibly irrationally, but in a collective action which had not been organized, a sort of spontaneous boycott. People realized that they could recover power though their shopping and their consumption. It was a significant new development, as we see in the growth of farm shops, and even of organic farming, where what people are buying are basic products. These mean they have to set to work and offer their family something of themselves, however little, by turning these products into dishes that are appetizing and good to eat.

Such a change of attitude could lead to a new approach to livestock farming. People would no longer simply buy 'beef' but a particular meat, a piece of living flesh with a specific character. Not all cuts of beef are good for the same purpose, and meat is not simply mince or steak, which people buy without knowing what it is. For decades supermarket customers have believed they were buying bull meat when what they were being sold were pieces of cull cow. There has been both a nutritional and a gustatory loss in the case of meat. People imagined they were buying a staple food when what they were actually buying was a standardized product; vacuum-packed minced meat is an extreme case. The hamburger is the classic example of the standardization of different products and so an excellent symbol of a whole food process-ing system based on *trompe l'oeil* and deception. The customer is also deceived by the false reassurance offered by the term 'traceability'. The origin of the meat is not a sufficient guarantee in itself; everything depends on the way the animals are reared. There is little point in knowing that it is a certain farmer who produced the meat if you have no way of knowing how he did it. None of this is enough in itself, if you do not remember that for an animal to be well grown and for the meat to be good, the beast has to have lived for a certain period of time. In other words, livestock farming has to change.

When visiting dairy farms in the United States José Bové was amazed to be told that a cow there has on average two calves in its life.

The cull rate in intensive production in the United States is such that a cow calves on average only twice in its lifetime. And it may be slaugh-tered before, because it is got rid of if its yield falls. Farming is now so intensive and the number of animals so great that meat is no longer seen as something to be built up but as a by-product of the dairy industry.

In France, a cow usually calves four or five times, which is in itself a relatively small number. It is regarded as unproductive to hold on to animals. The system has got out of control. For the herds of milk ewes in the Roquefort basin, rather more than 30 per cent of animals are culled annually. This is an incredibly high rate. Productivity is all that counts, in the case of both milk and meat. But mad cow disease is asso-ciated with intensive methods of milk production, since the feeds con-taining rendered animal remains that are at the heart of the problem were principally used in dairy herds to increase productivity. The cows were given protein-supplemented feed so that they would produce more milk, further proof that meat is no more than a typical by-product of intensive dairy farming. The activity has been perverted, and so has the job of the farmer. Mixed farming, where milk, meat and cereals to feed the livestock were produced, has been abandoned in favour of a system of extreme specialization that has as its sole purpose the generation of profit. The milk producer produces milk, the cereal grower grows cereals, the pig breeder breeds pigs, and so on. At the end of the day, there is no longer any autonomy on farms; decisions are made elsewhere. We no longer even talk of farms; we talk of production units.

7 An Economic Nonsense and an Ecological Aberration

Productivism in agriculture has taken us ever deeper into a high-risk world. Once you forget you are working with living things, you become disconnected from fundamentals and renounce your primary values; you play the sorcerer's apprentice. Foot-and-mouth disease in Europe offers an excellent example of how we have multiplied risks, because it is a disease linked to transport. Our parents lived through a similar epizootic outbreak some forty years ago. In those days, a farm usually had only six or eight animals, at most ten, and trade was largely local, conducted within the confines of the canton. Animals were driven on foot to the local weekly market, from within a distance of at most fifteen or twenty kilometres, and, except for the occasional exchange of a cow in calf between neighbours, you went to the cattle market. Livestock farming was then well under control. An epidemic of swine fever, caused by a virus that spreads through the air, was quickly contained, without giving rise to panics or irrational fears. A protection zone was declared and the animal was treated. Farmers attached an economic value to each beast, but also a sentimental value. They used disinfectants such as wheat bran; they put the animal's hoof in a canvas bag soaked in this substance, painted its mouth, and in four or five days the problem had gone away. The few animals that had been affected lost a little weight, and sometimes one died, but the storm eventually passed and within a few weeks was forgotten.

Today, the concentration of animals in a few huge establishments means cattle trucks have to travel long distances. The fact that animals are being daily transported all over the world considerably increases the risks. In the first place, the animals are enfeebled by being reared in a system designed to accelerate the growth of what are called 'cash cows'; livestock are pushed to their genetic limit. Second, it is now no longer unusual to transport animals 500, 1,000 or even 2,000 kilometres. Third, sanitary inspections have been halted in the name of liberalism. 'Trade rules.' Sensible protection, professional conscience and ethics – all such values have been abandoned and everything sacrificed on the altars of profit and business. Yet, at the same time, the beneficiaries of this system, the proponents of productivism, have taken good care not to be held responsible for its consequences. When there is a health scare, people's fears are quickly aroused, and politicians rush into action, anxious not to be accused at some later date of inertia. As a result, whole flocks and herds are burned, animals are slaughtered, and destruction is rife. As they watch the bonfires and the killing, farmers are made to realize the full extent of the transformation that has been forced on them; from being producers of food and foodstuffs, their prime vocation, they have become manufacturers of raw materials, of merchandise pure and simple, which is a violation of their original role. During these waves of irrational panic, at the height of these crises that cannot be allowed to continue, they may even find themselves turned into energy producers for cement manufacturers, since some of the carcasses are sent off to be used to heat cement works.

What were they supposed to have done? They earned more by filling in forms applying for subsidies than by spending their time on their tractors or tending their cows.

Forty years of such a process has stripped the basic elements from the farmer's job, the connection between the act of production, which consists of giving life, and the social act of eating and appreciating the value of our daily bread. These are both symbolic and civic values, which our parents taught us constituted respect for life.

One of the arguments put forward by the proponents of intensive agriculture is that small farmers are more exposed and more vulnerable to natural risks such as drought, storms, floods and epidemics.

The opposite is the case. Natural risks present a greater threat to the very large farms, where the size of fields has often been hugely increased, to the point of rendering the countryside featureless, and where monoculture rules. This creates problems with water retention in the soil and its humus content; with the loss of windbreaks, the leached soil becomes hard as concrete and at certain times of year is subject to run-off. When fields are enlarged and trees and hedges are grubbed up, the risks are all the greater. Small farms are much more stable thanks to their crop rotations, a more agronomic approach, and because lighter yields require fewer applications of chemical inputs. The land is permanently as if new. A farm that practises monoculture and has done away with its hedges is a worn-out farm, which will one day have to stop producing if it is to recover a meaning. If it is not rescued from this system, it will eventually grind to a halt of its own accord because the yields will fail on its sterile soils. Changes must be made in the very near future on these large farms; hedges and trees must be reintroduced, and crops cultivated that will restore agronomic value to the soil.

In livestock farming areas, on farms that practise crop rotation, a few cereals, beet, fodder cabbages and legumes introduced into the meadows maintain a permanently high humus content and an aerated soil, which is a good filter and which is in part nourished by the nitrogen in the air. The land is less difficult to work and less difficult to plough; it does not 'set', as they say; it neither sticks nor forms into clods. In a monoculture, there are no longer any barriers to natural catastrophes. The much-enlarged farms and the clearance of hedgerows represent, quite apart from the ecological dimension, an economic disaster for the nation, because these very farms, which have swallowed up so much in subsidies to facilitate their restructuring, remain permanently highly unstable. On farms devoted entirely to maize or to cereals, there are frequent water shortages and droughts; a few days or a few weeks of sun can fatally disrupt the crop and doom the yields. On farms where the soil is well balanced, on the other hand, one can be confident that the soils will not suffer in the same way from a hot spell or a rainstorm, and the crop will be less adversely affected. The blame can always be put on global warming and the rise in the water level. We have not yet seen the catastrophes some have predicted for future centuries. But it is certainly the case that the grubbing up of hedgerows and the disappearance of banks and trees explain why, in the winter of 2000, in just a few minutes or a few hours, villages were engulfed and houses flooded in a way never seen in the past.

When the harvest is bad, surely the budget of the small farmer is vulnerable whereas a large farmer can absorb the loss and survive?

When there is an extended period of drought, all farms will experience some difficult moments. That is why funding schemes need to be put in place – and funds for assistance in case of natural catastrophes exist – that are a charge both on the community and on farmers. But it is also important to try to match crop types to the nature of the soil, and to establish farming systems that are suited to the micro-climate and the expertise of the farmer, so that this sort of catastrophe can be avoided. It has become clear that the practice of growing cereals or maize irrespective of the type of soil, because of the subsidies, increases the need for irrigation. A soil that is heavily irrigated is a soil that is gradually being impoverished. It eventually becomes no more than a support for the crop. But if a fund is established to compensate for natural catastrophes, it should not be called on year in year out, whenever a particular soil fails to produce the anticipated yield.

Three or four years ago, we were invited by the Ministry of Agriculture to discuss what was called a 'mutual aid fund against economic hazards'. What it boiled down to was that, on the one hand, farmers were being asked to increase their production and reduce their costs, while, on the other, the community was being asked to assure the farmers an income every year if they failed to get a price that covered their expenses. The idea is surreal. Such a system would free farmers from all responsibility, and remove their incentives, since there would be little point in them straining themselves if they were always going to be bailed out, while expecting the community to foot the bill for unwise political choices. We are opposed to such a scheme; this sort of insurance against calamity, a piece of economic madness that exists in the United States, is a veritable plague. We are not hostile to a system of support for the victims of calamities, but it must be kept within limits, and we cannot ignore the pressing need to revert to a type of agriculture where farmers don't grow just anything, anywhere, anyhow. Sadly, the CAP is encouraging farmers to practise monoculture for the world market. This is in spite of the considerable need for nitrogenous proteins to feed our livestock, France and Europe importing 70 per cent of these vegetable proteins. It would be perfectly possible to reintroduce legumes such as alfalfa and clovers into the meadows in regions of low fertility, and such a shift to crops less thirsty for water and better able to withstand drought would allow farmers to recover a degree of autonomy.

Is the solution for livestock farmers, or their neighbours, to produce their own vegetable proteins?

In the early 1960s a deal was struck between the United States and Europe during the discussions of the Treaty of Rome: 'Europe has a vocation to produce cereals and rear animals; the United States can produce vast quantities of nitrogenous proteins; on this basis, we can trade.' What nonsense! At the time, no one raised the issue of the overall energy cost of a development of this type, either in the United States or in Europe. We are now entering a new era. After our battle to stop the use of feedstuffs containing animal remains, now would be a good time to revise the Blair House accord of 1992 which ratified the agreements of 1958, by which Europe was restricted to growing 5 million hectares of vegetable proteins with financial support. It was therefore not in the farmers' interests to produce soya themselves, but rather to buy it from Third World countries. A 'protein plan' for Europe would involve the following measures: the freeing up of land currently lying fallow in Europe (between 2 and 4 million hectares); the freeing up of land currently used to produce a wheat surplus for the world market, which brings no return to the community but costs it dear (between 4.5 and 5 million hectares); the use of these two types of available land to produce vegetable proteins that are appropriate to Europe – soya in some regions, sunflowers in others, elsewhere flax or garden and fodder peas.

On his farm, near livestock farming areas, François Dufour has successfully tested the cereal mixture oats, wheat, triticale and peas.

The incorporation of fodder peas into this mixture produces a cattle feed that, while not perfectly balanced between nitrogenous substances and protein, is a vegetable combination that considerably reduces the need to buy soya cake, and so allows greater autonomy. There can be no doubt that if all farms did the same in dairy, pig or poultry farming areas, imports from abroad would be significantly reduced. This would bring enormous savings to the French and European budgets that are now burdened (to the benefit of the petrol-producing countries) with the energy costs of all the ships laden with soya that cross the Atlantic from the Americas and return with cargoes of surplus wheat. Nor should we forget the fuel consumed by ships sailing to the Middle East, or the diesel consumed by lorries transporting cheap industrial chicken meat. There has been a notable lack of enthusiasm for calculating these energy costs. France has invested so heavily in autoroutes and lorry transport that a whole industry is now dependent on farming, which it sees as a milch cow. The beneficiaries of this system have no desire to see it changed. But the gigantic deficit cannot be ignored.

We face an intolerable paradox. The more expensive farming is to Europe, the more its farmers' incomes fall. If this was a price that had to be paid in the interests of one's country, or to achieve better food, enhanced protection for the countryside, and the growth of rural tourism, the taxpayer would be able to say: 'At least, what I am giving does some good.' But the CAP, it must be repeated, spends money like water and is an economic nonsense.

8 The Agricultural 'Titanic'

Is the CAP an infernal machine that is by now unstoppable, a beast forever doomed to chase its own tail? Or is it a means to an end, that is, the demise of anything that opposes the laws of the international market? Is it part of a policy aimed at the gradual and ineluctable extinction of the small farmer, on the pretext that no society can function by going into reverse? If there is a final purpose, beyond 'production for production's sake', it is the creation of a France with no more than 250,000 peasant farmers. What future awaits us if the CAP continues unchanged?

Let us begin with the example of England, a country which no longer has an extensive and diverse agriculture. In the early 1980s – that is, in the Thatcher era – England chose to enter European agriculture in force by lowering production costs and dismantling anything that was a financial drain on livestock farming; there were to be no more public services, no more veterinary services, no more controls, no more identification. Local abattoirs were shut down in favour of huge slaughterhouses in certain regions. At the same time, it was decided that England should be the centre for the import of lamb from New Zealand and Australia. This policy, it was hoped, would make the English masters of Europe; like the United States, they would trade on a grand scale and lay all other countries low, even bleed them dry. Sadly for the English, as successive crises have shown, the system has blown up in their faces, a fit reward for such a reckless approach to the management of living things.

The situation is currently unresolved. The number of small farmers in England, already less than 1 per cent of the population, will soon fall to 0.2 or 0.3 per cent; only a handful, a few tens of thousands, will survive. As a result, farming is likely to become even more intensive and even more dangerous, as there will be no one to manage it, and herds may expand to as large as one or two thousand sows, five thousand ewes, or seven or eight hundred cows. The health situation will then be even more precarious than before the recent crises; a disaster of titanic proportions threatens.

The only way to save farming in England would be to go back to farms on a human scale, restore the lost public services, and establish identification systems, health controls and a government department that did its job and saw agriculture as a means both of managing land and of providing employment. Alas, everything suggests that nothing will change, under a Conservative or a Labour government, and that farming will continue its headlong rush to destruction by pushing the system to its limits, on the American model.

France is heading in the same direction, in the longer or shorter term, because it is failing to help its small farmers. It is allowing the restructuring gradually to continue, and its farmers are leaving the land. By continuing to give generous subsidies to farming on the great plains and in the principal cereal zones, it is aggravating the budgetary deficit. Is France going to take England as its model? Will we, in ten years' time, have reached the same point?

José Bové and François Dufour together visited an England in shock, and here describe what they found.

In France we have the good fortune to live in a land of great diversity. In June 2001 I visited England with José Bové; 97 per cent of agriculture in that country is called into question by mad cow disease, foot-and-mouth disease, and the intensification of cereal farming. A mere 3 per cent is organic, and there is nothing between the two. In France, by contrast, we retain a diversified agriculture, in the mountains, the plains, the humid zones, the hot, dry regions, and all the various micro-climates. In Britain, radical changes are needed. At our meetings, farmers told us how much needed to be done, but said they lacked popular support. Consumers kept telling them that they had stopped eating meat because of mad cow and foot-and-mouth disease. Furthermore, as English cereals lack outstanding qualities, people have completely changed their eating habits and lost their taste; they have retreated, frightened of everything. England lacks the diversity of products, of regions, of fresh food, and of flavours that we are lucky to have in France.

'Farming is costing us dear,' concludes the English government, having faced one crisis after another. Tourism, they observe, is much more profitable. Do we, then, they ask, still need to support agriculture? What they are really thinking is: if we can rely on the world market for our food, do we really need small farmers?

This Blairite economic reasoning ignores unemployment in its calculations, no longer seeing jobs as a priority. There are many countries, for that matter, that have abandoned this particular criterion; even in France, when we argue the case for farming as a provider of employment, many politicians appear resigned to ignoring this issue.

Those who proselytize on behalf of profitability forget that the management of the natural world, including keeping animals in the most difficult regions, and the management of the landscape go hand in hand with the management of tourism. A diversified country like France, with all its beaches to be cleaned and maintained, all its mountains, all its tourist and leisure centres, and its summer resorts and winter sports stations, cannot manage without farming. Whatever people say, it would be impossible today to find the labour simply to see to the upkeep of open spaces. Taking lawnmowers into the low, medium and high mountains would be a good deal more costly to the nation and hardly solve the problem. It is simply not practicable to dispense with the three missions of a localized farming: production, employment and conservation.

The idea that a country can buy its food on the world markets, dispense with its farms, and rely on job creation schemes for young people and pensioners to maintain its waters, its soils and its landscape is an economic nonsense. In France, we are already seeing the cost of abandoning all the difficult soils in the precarious zones, where land is lying fallow and a jungle of brambles and undergrowth emerging. At first, farmers go on ploughing the neighbouring fields, but eventually they realize that it is no longer profitable. If the logic is pushed even further, as in England, whole regions will be wiped off the map. The result will be, quite apart from the social costs of caring for those who will be left jobless, a loss to our heritage, a degradation of the countryside, and a slump in rural tourism, which is currently poised for growth. Nor should we forget the cost of the pollution, the epidemics and the health scares. The further we push the intensification of industrial agricultural production, the more we create monsters that will return to haunt us. At the end of the day, we face a farming 'Titanic'.

This doomsday scenario does not apply only to relatively well-off countries like France, or Europe as a whole, but also to the developing countries. Large-scale exports will cause the ruin of local agricultures and do nothing to solve the problem of world hunger or the diseases associated with malnutrition. If subsistence farming is destabilized and then abandoned, more and more people will migrate to the cities and the shanty towns. For the industrialized countries and the productivist sectors, the aim is to create new markets. To create these in the big cities and the great capitals means removing new populations from the land that supports them, assembling them, and turning them into consumers of mass-produced products.

Thanks to this massive migration, the food processing industry is anticipating a 3 per cent annual growth. It would be salutary to design an electronic map that would show in red the drift of populations from the rural to the urban areas, that is, to a regime of fast food. We would be able to see the full extent of the red on the planet. The red zones would equal overpopulation, insecurity, acculturation and, eventually, conflict. All the land that is now lying waste will only be productive in future for industrial agriculture. The Landless Movement in Brazil is fighting to gain access to land, but the rich landowners have no wish to surrender their uncultivated estates. The land in question is very fertile, and they are waiting for the arrival of agribusiness and the offer of incentives to grow crops for export.

If we pursue this doomsday scenario to the very end, we can visualize a world in which food wars are general and are won by agribusiness, where everyone will receive a single meal, and it will be the same wherever you are. Standardizing and making everything uniform will be the end of thinking, the end of action, and the end of everything. But how convenient for agribusiness! If we were all to eat the same thing, in the same quantities, we could all buy our rations from vast depots. We can see this happening already in the case of huge production companies like Sodexo, which supplies food to mass caterers. According to the menu of the day, 800,000, a million, even one and a half million people are all eating, for example, beef, carrots and peas that have been produced by the same firm. And since even the rich are now spending less of their money on food, they will be eating the same as everyone else.

The earliest firm date for the reform of the CAP is 2006. The power of the lobbies is such that they are succeeding in preventing this date from being brought forward. A mid-term revision is fiercely opposed. What will be the consequences if current policy is maintained until at least 2006?

The CAP has based its development on a system of total standardization and the production of primary materials as cheaply as possible. Its subsidies are administered with this aim in view, and the CAP presses ahead in defiance of what society wants, which is an agriculture that provides employment, that preserves, and that produces foodstuffs of high quality. These fundamental choices must be reversed. If nothing changes in the next ten or twenty years, we will be well on the way towards an agriculture wholly in the hands of the agro-chemistry industry, with no more small farmers. This will mean the loss of acquired tastes, the whole population being accustomed to uniform flavours; the tax burden, meanwhile, will continue to increase. We need to decide – and here governments must play their part – whether food is something fundamental to society or whether we are going to allow agribusiness to take over. The crucial issue is: the weapon of food. We know how many people there are in a country, we know how much food they need year on year, and, whatever the climatic or political vagaries, we know how much has to be produced. The facts are available. They are known to governments. The statistics have existed for many years, and they cannot be far wrong. The crucial question, therefore, is to know whether the food weapon is going to continue to be entrusted to agribusiness or whether it is the triptych of jobs, land and production that will at last come first.

If we do not switch to a different agricultural policy, the whole of farming will fall into the hands of the five agro-chemical groups that dominate the world. When the planet is totally polluted, several decades from now, where will we find the farmers with the fundamental values to re-enter this profession? It will be necessary to relearn, over a long period of time, what sort of agriculture is needed for the future. If we are to avoid this situation, it is urgent that the CAP changes direction and that action is taken to ensure that it is not the WTO that sets the farming agenda. It is for individual countries or groups of countries to determine their own degree of food self-sufficiency and to exercise the right to choose their own farming methods, regulate issues of food safety and health, and reject certain practices. Trade should be organized in a way that respects and encourages the capacity of each country to feed itself from within its own frontiers.

In the doomsday scenario of a continuation of this policy to the benefit of a few multinationals, farmers will be no more than industrial workers, though a few of them might get jobs as regional park keepers, complete with uniform and shiny badge.

Such changes would be to institutionalize a two-tier agriculture and the worst of all possible compromises. But farming could very easily be reoriented towards quality and regional products by means of financial incentives. The existing European Union budget, which is substantial, could be utilized to encourage a number of changes in the immediate future. If assistance and support were injected into a regional agriculture with high added value, it would give an immediate boost to those small farmers who are still in business and who could pass on their knowledge of the job. In other words, changes could be made within the existing budget. If this is not done, a two-tier agriculture will prevail: on the one hand, a handful of producers of quality for the rich; on the other, industrial farming for the poor, practised by farmers whose income consists entirely of public assistance and subsidies. It would be a tragedy. We must tackle the problem today, without delay, while France still retains some 600,000 farms, a good half of which are on a human scale and worked by people who have skills and who retain values of which they are the repositories and custodians: local breeds of cattle, strains of seeds, a land adapted to micro-climates, and a landscape linked to history.

Are the traditional family farms of our neighbours, the Dutch, the Flemish and the Belgians, disappearing at the same rate as in France?

In the current situation, the number of farms is falling at the same rate more or less everywhere in the European Union, though even more rapidly in the south. Why is this happening? The six main countries have enjoyed eighty-three years of life in common, from 1958 to 2001. These are countries where modernization and agricultural development have made great strides; they were so far ahead that when the southern countries – that is, Greece, Portugal, Spain and Italy, where the farms are very small – joined this increasingly organized – or disorganized – European market, they suffered badly in the subsequent maelstrom. The farms that produced foodstuffs with high added value and marketed their produce locally were able to withstand the pressure. But those that were subjected to the turbulence of the market in cereals, milk, meat or vegetables found themselves, for the most part, in a disastrous situation. Thousands of such farms went under. The proportion of peasant farmers in the European Union varies, according to country, from 1 per cent (or even less in the United Kingdom) to 12 per cent (in Greece and Portugal), but even there it is shrinking fast, and will soon be down to 5 per cent or less. It is a tragedy, because these countries, which have serious social problems, are banking on a growth of tourism, and it is only in cohabitation with farming that tourism will continue to generate employment. If agriculture is allowed to collapse, tourism will collapse too. The CAP has the same effect everywhere, so the whole of Europe is in the same mess.

9 How to Emerge from the Crisis: A Diagnosis and the Beginnings of a Cure

How are we to respond to those who say that the machine is running at full tilt, that it has reached a point of no return, and that even if we have to compensate for its pernicious consequences, it is too late to put the clock back? How are we to convince people that, on the contrary, there is still time to reform the CAP, and that the timetable must be brought forward, not only in order to lessen the pernicious consequences, but also to change direction, and to try to recover peasant memory, that reservoir of experience and storehouse of knowledge dating back to a time when contact with the soil was primordial.

To accept that industrialized agriculture has reached a point of no return is to accept that those in the driving seat of the CAP are no longer capable of applying the brakes when asked to do so by the majority of their passengers, and that the machine is running out of control.

Let us remember that the alienation of small farmers happened in three stages. First, they stopped preparing the land for sowing according to the condition and content of the soil and climatic conditions, and began to do what they were told by their co-operative. Then they were supplied with a piece of paper that told them the approximate dates for using a certain number of chemicals and the types to use, by which time they had lost their knowledge based on experience. Last they reached the stage found in many countries of the world, and especially in the United States, where the computer took over; a computer program explained to farmers that they had to become part of the system and seek the advice of an external consultant if they wanted to produce what the market demands.

How can we break out of these repeated crises?

Without waiting for 2006, we can make a start by taking certain measures, changing our practices, and adopting an initial set of reforms.

First, we need to revitalize the soils. For this we need a soil survey and an inventory of resources. These would almost certainly reveal why we need to stop causing damage, polluting and impoverishing the soils, and why we are experiencing floods, sudden rainstorms and so on, and also that sufficient resources exist in French soil to put things right. What is happening is not inevitable; the process is reversible. If we want to change course and pursue different objectives, we need to redefine the bases of production to make them respond to the needs of society as a whole. The first question is this: what sort of foodstuffs do we want, in what quantity, and of what quality? The second: can society exist on cheap foodstuffs alone? No, no more than it can live without recovering a sense of what is natural. Given that the configuration of the landscape is the work of human beings, the degradation of the soils and the problems of erosion are in part a consequence of public policies. We need to question the scientists: are the soil, the subsoil and the groundwater, in their present condition, likely to preserve over the long term the health of humans and that of animals and plants? Certainly not. And what bases and fundamental principles do we lay down for the management of the soil, the subsoil and the groundwater in order to respond to the needs of society? The answers to these questions may amount to a new global plan for agriculture: does the social tie that exists between farmers and the rest of society serve a purpose? If the countryside is deserted, what are the consequences for society? If it is in the general interest for the countryside to be populated, how is this to be achieved? Should we simply create dormitory suburbs? No, because in that case neither the countryside nor the land will be maintained. If, on the contrary, the best solution is to keep small farmers in every region, we need to find ways of redistributing agricultural production and of restoring all its meaning to the job of the farmer.

Once agreement on these points is reached in Brussels, what methods and how much time will be needed for the following policies to be implemented: an increase in the number of farm set-ups, the creation of more farms than are abandoned, an end to concentration, the encouragement of farms of medium size, a limit to pig production, an end to the pollution of groundwater, the restoration of hedgerows and tree planting, the recovery of abandoned land to grow vegetable proteins, and so on. Given the current situation, and if we do our stocktaking, is this possible and how long will it be before we see results?

At present, about 5 per cent of the foodstuffs produced in Europe enter the global market, and this 5 per cent, which brings nothing into the community, dictates 95 per cent of agricultural production for the internal markets of the European Union. This 5 per cent also depresses prices and puts one small farmer in three in an impossible position; there comes a point at which he is forced to abandon his land and his crops to the benefit of the two who survive. This has been happening now for some forty or fifty years. We must break out of this system. Once it is understood that the food self-sufficiency of populations implies the continued survival of farming in every continent, we are in a position to change the political choices at the European level; we can decide that if a proportion of production is put on the world market, it should not be subsidized. In other words, public money should not be used to finance a tool that works against the community and its small farmers. Once we cease to subsidize the proportion destined for export, we will be well on the way to solving not only the budgetary problem but also global social problems. We can change the direction of the machine in the very short term if only we abandon this infernal race.

If we free up public assistance and stop financing the global market, how should the funds that are released be used? We propose that we start from the fact that the regions and their products vary hugely; the vagaries of the climate and the problems associated with local weather conditions, harsh seasons, and the nature of the soils, some more difficult to work than others, constitute handicaps unknown in the regions of high agricultural potential and easy growth. Public support should be concentrated on the less favoured regions, compensating for the natural, climatic, labour and agronomic handicaps.

If all these aspects are taken into account, the job of the farmer will once again be a noble undertaking.

Do we need to reinstate protective measures to control the circulation of merchandise?

Yes. Not in order to close frontiers but to retain a degree of control – for example, reinstating customs duties in certain sectors.

Once the system of subsidies is reformed, should we immediately abandon factory farming, or opt for a sensible compromise? Should factory farming be abolished outright or improved?

We should certainly stop administering drugs to livestock, to avoid potential hazards. But to return to an agriculture that was unproductive would be irresponsible and is wholly undesirable. It would, on the other hand, be possible progressively to embark on a rapid de-intensification, for example, to take measures that would allow poultry to lead a more natural life. There is no question of returning to the hen-house with four or five hens and a couple of pullets. But we do need to return to norms of animal health that are accepted by veterinary surgeons experienced in the specialized rearing of poultry or pigs. We are not advocating pig farming out in the open, because to put pigs outside is not a panacea, and no one wants to see a return to the old days. But there is no reason why we should not get rid of the concrete floors and keep pigs on a litter of sawdust or straw. The advocates of sustainable farming are currently experimenting with a system for rearing pigs, which is going well; it would be possible to help this type of farming to become competitive. The aim is to break away from industrial livestock farming behind closed doors; there should be a gradual return to more controllable methods by reducing the number of animals per square metre, by making buildings conform to new animal welfare norms, by protecting the animals' health, and by rationalizing the way they are fed. In sum, we should aim to ensure a global management of flocks or herds over the long term, as opposed to the short-term expedient of industrial livestock farming.

How should the land be used?

The agriculture of the future will be viable if farms operate more autonomously and more genuinely economically. Farmers will have to assume greater control over the production of their fodders so that they are able to guarantee total transparency in the provenance of the foodstuffs they produce. That is why it is desirable that they go back to growing as many fodder crops as possible on their own fields and keep tight control over their production. Crop rotation was abandoned during all those years when specialization and monoculture were seen as the universal panacea. The consequences of growing legumes on soils for decades while simultaneously growing cereals and grasses alongside in a monoculture are disastrous, whereas crop rotation with grasses and legumes, either together or alternately, keeps the soil well balanced, evacuates toxins, and reduces colonies of predators. Farmers have a double interest in planting forage crops, both to feed their livestock and to avoid monoculture. If all this were combined, significant savings could be made in the use of the fertilizers and the chemicals that are necessary in a monoculture, as in factory farming.

What about the trade in meat and live beasts?

This trade is a nonsense, economically and socially. To produce an animal protein, seven vegetable proteins are needed. Do we really need to eat so much meat? Nutritionists ought to look at this question with a view to recommending balanced meals and a balanced diet for the population as a whole.

Whatever the pros and cons of a carnivorous diet, to have huge quantities of exported meat traversing the planet is economic nonsense, given that every country has the capacity to produce its own meat. We need to take a fresh look at international trade on the basis of national food self-sufficiency. The trade will then adjust itself. Let us therefore stop exporting our meat to the sub-Saharan countries, in effect dumping it, thanks to the subsidies, so as to avoid ruining the economies of those countries; and let us stop importing beef from Argentina and lamb from New Zealand for everyone in Europe to eat.

People go to American restaurant chains as a family because they have separate eating areas and play areas for children.

These chains are seeking to expand throughout the world in order to maximize profits from their raw materials. The meats currently used by most of these firms are of very poor quality, and they are produced by farmers who no longer make a profit. It is another example of the failure of free-market globalization, which wanted, indeed still wants, to standardize every sector of activity at the lowest level and put them in permanent competition, recognizing neither the right to work nor the right to have production costs taken into account. The market in Argentinian beef is profitable only because the cattle are pumped full of hormones.

This fierce competitiveness is impoverishing not only the planet and society but also the bodies and souls of consumers. If we respected fundamental principles, and if we put a stop to globalization and reinstated trade barriers, it would end. When people no longer want to eat at home or cook for themselves, the family begins to disintegrate. Those citizens who resign themselves to this fate are condoning the failure of a system and hardly preparing a bright future for their children. They are complicit in a sort of doctrine of universal alienation. They must realize this, and soon.

Faced with the competition of the big pig producers, small farmers should perhaps diversify into making their own cooked pork meats, and compensate for falling pig sales by the added value of farm-produced goods.

There is a huge potential market for locally produced foodstuffs with high added value; it will be necessary, however, for all the ingredients and the costs of traditional manufacture to be set out in a handbook of good practice that can be consulted at the butcher's shop or supermarket.

Farmers have for years allowed others to collect this added value, and they bear their share of responsibility for the present state of affairs. Why did they let themselves be exploited in this way? In the early 1960s, when the growth of co-operatives and producer groups was getting under way, it made sense to pool their means of production to act as a counterweight to certain industries. The watchword then was: 'We are producers not processors, and we can't do everything.'

At that period, farmers trusted the big companies to market their produce, but in the space of thirty or thirty-five years the situation has been transformed. The farmers have let the added value elude them altogether; they have become mere manufacturers of cheap primary materials. Now that their position has been strengthened by greater public awareness as a result of the repeated health scares, they need to develop other ways of processing and marketing their produce so that they can retain the added value; the consumer, too, might benefit if all the intermediaries could be dispensed with. At present, in certain sectors, the cost of the basic product accounts for less than 10 per cent of the total cost of the finished item. There are even instances where the cost of packaging and advertising comes to three times that of the product itself, and the cost of transport to between four and six times. The profit margins left to the farmers are ridiculous, and they are no longer being paid for their work. They will have to devise alternatives. Farmers could combine, for example, to establish a unit for processing their produce in common. If the farmers themselves were unable to provide the necessary capital to set up small-scale processing and marketing units, consumer groups might be able to make a contribution. Whatever the contract agreed, it is essential that there is something for everybody and that everybody is fairly paid. This might also be a way to develop links with the consumer that are lasting, coherent and transparent. It reveals the need for a prior collective debate on the subject of what the citizen wants the farmer to supply for their three meals a day. The fact that the big names have captured the market means that new types of contacts between citizens and farmers will have to be devised. This is the only way that small farms can be given new life. They should not be aiming to sell their produce cheaply in competition with industrialized agriculture in supermarkets, 98 per cent of whose trade is in the hands of the international companies. They will have to establish new contacts. These products of high added value could give a boost to local markets at every level and increase their number, as long as the financial measures and administrative and legal regulations give this category of producers a chance.

In the context of globalization, draconian standards are imposed on small producers who are without the financial means to implement them, and no distinction is made between products that have substance and products made precarious by industrial methods. We should remember that thirty years ago our parents hung their bacon from the ceiling and kept a boiling fowl in a meat-safe for days on end. Why did these meats keep perfectly well in a cool temperature at a time when there were no refrigerators? Because this was meat that had been produced much more slowly, that had substance, and that did not go off. Today, if you buy a slice of industrial meat and leave it for a few minutes in front of a sunny window, you are asking for trouble from bacteria. A certificated high-quality or organic product, on the other hand, will keep much better. We have to find a new way of talking to consumers. We have to explain that products may cost more than they do today; but that they can expect this to be balanced against a reduction in price as distribution and processing networks are shortened, and the number of intermediaries along the line reduced; and that if agriculture is revitalized in this way, they may also feel the benefit when they calculate their taxes, because they will no longer have to pay what they have paid in the past to repair the damage caused by productivism.

Is it realistic to think in terms of the abolition of slurry-spreading rights or of pigs being put out to grass once again?

There are other ways of rebuilding sustainable production. Sows and their piglets could be reared on soil and then fattened in buildings which used different types of litter, even soil. Many different production methods are now being tried out. The immensely powerful pig lobby has seen the growth of intensive production as a way of keeping the cement industry in business, by selling ready-made buildings with integral flooring or cesspit. Meanwhile the energy industry sells ventilation systems and engineering firms sell slurry-spreaders to get rid of the liquid manure.

The government has accepted this state of affairs under pressure from the pig lobby, which has had an interest in keeping the system going for many years.

Environmental constraints will force a shift to sustainable pig farming. We are now being told that producers, especially in the west of France, are installing new purifiers for the liquid manure. It is the same old story, like the factory that pollutes a river and then spends a fortune on a purifying unit so that it can go on polluting.

For several decades now, water has been seen as a source of profit like any other, rather than as a common property of humanity, and no one has bothered to enquire whether the supply might one day dry up. Nothing has been done to protect either the quality or the quantity of this resource. Artesian wells have been sunk and pumps installed without authorization, and the groundwater of others has been diverted, all in total anarchy. No one has been looking at what was going on underneath, nor has anyone wanted to ask who owned the subsoil. Once the groundwater has been destroyed, the farmers themselves no longer have access to this resource to water their own livestock; their production costs increase when they have to pay for the treatment or purchase of water. But they have also created a health risk of major proportions, which the system designed by the proponents of intensive farming cannot eliminate with the de-pollution techniques from which they make a profit. While this has been happening, the politicians have completely failed to do their job in protecting water resources. The value of the water, a common property of humanity, has never been a factor in the debate. When livestock units have been extended, questions might have been asked about the proximity of the buildings to private houses, or the likelihood of the prevailing winds carrying the smell to such and such a village, but no one has bothered to find out if the area was seriously vulnerable or not. The majority of the livestock units that no longer have water fit to drink now have a de-nitrification plant. The equipment is extremely expensive and solves nothing in the long term. If these units go on being used for many more decades, a catastrophe will surely follow.

It is a dangerous business. The construction of treatment stations (which is subsidized by public money) encourages the concentration of production on the same sites. This denatures agriculture and turns it into an industry.

Yet another example of a blind act of faith in technology: don't worry, says the pig lobby, we may not be going to cut production but we are going to clean up our act with the aid of a new generation of purifiers.

In opting for a slurry system of livestock farming, we have landed ourselves with a major problem of disposal. If we had chosen instead to concentrate on the use of straw, which absorbs liquid and which aerates and enriches the soil when dug into it as manure, we would have been spared the current problems of slurry-spreading. Furthermore, the land round the pig houses could have been fertilized for the growing of crops. The system has never been considered from this agronomic or ecological standpoint, but only from within an industrial logic. Liquid manure chills the soil; to warm it up, chemicals have to be applied. Furthermore, huge machines are required to spread the slurry. It consumes even more energy if it is decided not to spread the slurry locally. So the storage pits and tanks are further enlarged, and the slurry is transported in lorries. Who cares if they are then driven half-way across France? Action must be taken to reduce the number of animals kept in pig sheds in several regions, beginning with the very largest operations; new standards should be set to encourage farmers gradually to switch to manure-based rather than slurry systems. Little by little, we could return to the practice of husbanding resources and stop having to build de-nitrification plants.

Industrialized farming stands accused of polluting the atmosphere by crop spraying (with the use of aircraft in the case of the biggest fields), and by the destruction of neighbouring woodland. If small farming is revitalized, what will be its contribution to preserving the atmosphere?

A type of farming capable of evolving according to the needs of society would use chemicals wisely; it would even tend to avoid their use. Where cereals are grown, viticulture residues could be put on the soil, making chemical fertilizers superfluous. This would involve the soil being prepared and changes in the chemical treatments offered to farmers. When, for example, a death's head has been placed on a container, it should be inconceivable for such a dangerous product to be applied with sprays that project vapour into the air that will be breathed by local people and may adversely affect the local flora and fauna. Certain methods must be prohibited. Spraying by aircraft or helicopter, as happens in some countries, is truly scandalous. Farmers must be persuaded to use an integrated package of other practices so that they can avoid resort to these 'bombs'. In the present specialized systems, farmers have been trained to follow a treatment schedule that increasingly distances them from their fields. The old system whereby groups of farmers met up locally with a competent expert to discuss what they were about to do, and were encouraged to think about their practices, might usefully be revived. All dogmatism is to be avoided, but anything is valuable that leads to the use of more natural methods – for example, strengthening the immunity of a plant or a soil by enriching it with calcium or trace elements, or the anticipation or avoidance of catastrophes. If the molecules that are on offer are dangerous, it is incumbent on public research to come up with options that present no threat to health. Some farmers have opted for organic farming or biodynamics. Atmospheric pollution ought to be reduced in all sectors; it is inconceivable that we continue to spray so many insecticides and pesticides.

Intensive farming uses different compost from extensive farming, which can call on animal manure. We need to remember that the secret of the best manure lies in the feed given to the animals.

Manure is an important element for the soil because it is a way of aerating it, building up its microbic life, and increasing its capacity to provide the plant with the humus and nitrogen it needs. The type of animal feed influences the nature of the faecal matter. If animals have been fed a balanced and non-intensive diet, their dung will be much less aggressive for the soil. But if the animals are given only silage and concentrates, the dung will have a different structure from how it would be if they were given unrefined fodders, starches and cereal proteins. To make compost, the dung has to be left to break down without losing any of its richness and quality. The height and the width of the heap are important, as the dung has to breathe. If the heap is too compacted, too high or too dense, it will not mature and may even lose its stored nitrogen because it burns in the open air. A dung heap has to incorporate plenty of hay to be able to mature of its own accord and retain a sufficient degree of humidity. The presence of bacteria in the manure accelerates the process. All these elements combine to make compost that is good for the soil. A green manure, however, brought out of a building and put straight onto the land, has a damaging effect, chilling the soil and checking plant growth because it has not had enough light to develop. That is why it is necessary to remove the muck from the animal sheds and leave it to turn into compost during the winter out in the open.

The quality of plants, therefore, can depend indirectly on the feed given to the livestock. When the milk or the meat that people consume comes from cattle fed naturally, the latter's waste and discharges are also a source of future wealth. If milk is produced intensively, the food is degraded and so is the dung, hence the compost will not have the same quality. Yet, if used at the right time, according to the season of the plants under cultivation, well-composted manure is a gold-mine for the future crop.

In the reform of the CAP, what will be the role of crop rotation?

The CAP ought to rethink its farming support and redirect its subsidies with a view to encouraging a return to crop rotation. Given the right training, farmers would rediscover the roots and the sources of their profession. If Europe stopped subsidizing the ensilage of maize and encouraged the cultivation of fodder crops instead, farmers would make much more use of the land under grass than they do today. It would be in their interest to grow crops that would last for five or ten years rather than to plough the meadows every year. Achieving a balance on their land and adopting less aggressive practices that are less harmful to the environment would become instinctive to the farmer again.

Do we need a new policy with regard to fallow land?

In regions where access to farming is increasingly difficult because supposedly non-viable, the CAP has favoured leaving land uncultivated. But it has done the same in regions like the pays d'Auge, where farmhouses have been sold to English, Irish and Dutch purchasers, and the best land taken over by farmers from ten, fifteen or even twenty kilometres away. In this 'Suisse normande', where the countryside is beautiful and well kept, and where the half-timbered houses are easy to sell, emptiness has engendered emptiness, and the abandoned land has accelerated the desertification caused by the death of so many farms and the inactivity of the farming sector. The presence of residents for one month in the year will not breathe new life into a dead region. And a region that no longer plans for its future has no future.

Would it be possible to reintroduce the cultivation of plant proteins on this land?

Nitrogenous proteins can be grown in every region of France and Europe. In livestock farming areas, the farmers should make every effort to meet their own needs for proteins. But it is far from easy to change twenty-five or thirty years of specialization. A start could be made by the reintroduction into the meadows of legumes such as clovers and alfalfas, plants which are extremely rich in nitrogenous proteins, which store up natural nitrogen by fixing that in the atmosphere, and at the same time help the grasses and cereals to take in food. In these regions, it would be better to reduce the number of animals, use the land to produce proteins, and so buy less from outside. The arithmetic is easy. The reintroduction of legumes so as to lessen dependence on the world market would also give a boost to crop rotations. After two, three or four years of legumes, such as clovers in the meadows, cereals or maize could be grown for a year or two without nitrogen. There would be an overall saving. And farmers would be returning to the job that used to be theirs, operating more autonomously and more economically and once again producing added value.

In France, every region could produce its own proteins. These could be flax, rape, soya, lupins or sunflowers. Sunflowers and soya are best avoided in the north and the east of France, and should be grown where there is plenty of sun and the soils are favourable.

Protein plans adapted to the region would have an immediate positive all-round effect. If fewer animals were reared in the west of France, there would be a more even distribution of livestock in other regions. If legumes were reintroduced on to the soils of Brittany, fewer kilometres would be driven by lorries and fewer miles sailed by ships importing soya from Brazil or cassava from Thailand, or certain nitrogenous proteins from the south of France or southern Europe. It would be a return to a farming that was more 'socially correct' in relation to other countries and more economically viable for France itself.

François Dufour reintroduced legumes on his farm in Manche. As a result, he needed to buy between eighteen and twenty tons less of soya and between ten and twelve tons less of chemical fertilizers.

The leguminous plants on my land – white clovers and fodder peas in my cereals – are my contribution to the Europe-wide protein plan and to the reduction of lorry traffic. Surely it is better to have more small farmers, more local trade, and fewer huge lorries on the roads than a handful of long-distance lorry drivers, with trucks even longer than those in the United States, and an almost complete absence of farmers? Such reasoning is not backward-looking; on the contrary, it is taking account of all the global aspects of what society expects from farming.

Can the farming community really be trusted to look after the land, and provide the necessary treatment for soils that are in need of regeneration? With regard to water, two questions arise. First, are we not doing too much watering at a time when viewers are being asked on television to turn off the tap while they are cleaning their teeth? Don't use too much water, don't waste water, is the constant refrain. Surely the real over-use is the watering of so many fields, in particular in Beauce? The second question concerns the pollution of groundwater. What action can be taken to correct the present situation?

The mere fact of moving away from monoculture and instituting crop rotations will reduce water consumption. Why has the Adour basin specialized in the production of maize grains and seed and the Parisian basin become a wheat monoculture? Because a powerful industry has developed in the background. After all, if other crops were to be reintroduced into the Parisian basin, there would be no need to import manure from Finistère or the Côtes d'Armor. Livestock could gradually be reintroduced here, not to be kept in sheds, as in other regions, but on a different system. It would be easy, meanwhile, to introduce plants such as legumes, in combination with various other crops. Specialization in wheat for export to the other side of the world precludes such combinations. But if the Parisian basin still wants to have a local market, which could be Brittany with its pigs and its poultry, why not grow a combination of oats, wheat and fodder peas? The pea is leguminous, and by converting atmospheric nitrogen it would nourish the other plants. Such a crop rotation could be reintroduced gradually and would help to restore the desired balance.

Farming is not like a factory that is allowed to operate only as long as it is profitable; it is a long-term process, and you cannot switch systems from one day to the next. Once an irrigation system has been installed, the process cannot be reversed in the immediate short term; it remains necessary as long as there is a monoculture. The compacted soils need ever heavier watering to achieve higher yields, but the increase in productivity is not enough to pay for the irrigation, hence the grant of a European extra irrigation premium. This is a vicious circle, absurd at both the economic and the ecological levels. But we can gradually extricate ourselves from this situation, in particular by returning to crop rotations. The production of legumes would solve a number of problems at the same time.

Can the pollution of groundwater in France be blamed on productivist agriculture alone? In the west of France it is attributed to the concentration of pig farming, but groundwater has also been affected in other regions, where there is mixed farming.

All the ills of society cannot be blamed on farming. But the best way to manage the groundwater in the short run is to have available a concrete tool that would enable the farmer to be better informed about what is going on in the soil; for example, to employ a device capable of detecting the depth of the groundwater and the nature of the soils, to indicate what sort of crops the soil would be able to support.

Farming, like other sectors of society, has always discharged large quantities of waste and continues to do so. It was a great mistake to get rid of the filters that retained so much matter in the soil. When large numbers of cesspits were concreted so that slurry could be stored for longer periods, nothing was done about the problem of accumulating slurry in the soil. If we want to avoid this problem, the effluent could be put to good use if the filters that disappeared when drainage was installed were restored. Too little attention has been paid to the role of the humid zones and their capacity to retain polluting elements in the soil and transform them. The soils that became waterlogged in winter and the acid soils bearing grasses that were not easily accessible acted as filters. Everything was cleared out of the way with mechanical diggers in order to install drains, because this was a way to get your hands on a maize subsidy or a wheat subsidy. Drainpipes were laid right up to the edges of watercourses. Floods drain away all the chemical residues not absorbed by the maize. It is hardly surprising that it is now necessary to resort to palliatives such as de-nitrification circuits and water treatment plants. The policy was always mad.

Humid zones and areas with a lot of surface water need to be managed differently. The bias of the CAP has been so strong that it has even given subsidies for the growing of maize for silage on marshlands. The likelihood that catastrophic consequences would ensue within a decade in all these fragile zones described as at risk was ignored. In marshland where the grass has been there for decades, perhaps as long as a century, the roots combine to form a sort of carpet supporting vegetation and animals and helping to retain water. They are buffer zones that prevent flooding. Land has been drained without a thought for the consequences in terms of the speedier discharge of water. But the water has to go somewhere. And given the prospect of global warming, if we are already experiencing difficulties in dealing with the surplus water, how are we going to cope with rising levels in the future?

These marshy zones, which were defined a long time ago, had their own status, purpose and particularity. We should re-create these buffer zones, but not to make them into eco-museums; rather, they should continue to support a natural and controlled livestock farming that would be economically productive. We should stop ploughing up these lands for the sake of a monoculture dependent on the application of chemicals right up to the water's edge. We should stop the destruction of its rich carpet. In ploughing meadows in the marshes, thousands of tons of stored-up nitrogen have been released. As a general rule, manuring was unnecessary on these marshes. Large quantities of hay were produced in July, a second crop was grazed in September, and then the land was left to rest; its function was not reproduction but the evacuation of water and serving as a natural reserve, retaining water and preventing catastrophes such as those of the Baie de Somme and elsewhere.

We have upset the balance that both constituted the richness of our heritage and fulfilled an agro-economic function that a developed society owes it to itself to maintain. The Europe-wide Natura 2000 plan aims to protect zones, so we are told. A few plants and a few birds that nest there will be 'managed'. This scheme underestimates the importance of these buffer zones; the issue is not nature reserves but flood management. Natura 2000 is tackling the problem from a very narrow standpoint. The idea underlying the project is misguided; it encourages a rupture with civil society, which effectively wants these areas to be protected so that it can have the pleasure of visiting them. The danger is that they will be turned into living museums, whereas, for the small farmer, this is potentially productive land for fodder crops or for natural livestock farming. Let us have agricultural tourism, by all means, but not at the expense of agricultural productivity, which needs rebuilding in a sustainable way.

These are also zones where wealth is produced in winter and stored up for the spring. The waters that fleetingly take refuge there give the grass enormous taste and nutritional value. If animals are pastured there once more, we will rediscover quality products. The peasants of old knew that they served as reserves in case of fodder shortages, and from time to time they even sold hay in the interior if it was in short supply. The young farmers of today have not been trained in the management of these marshlands. People brought up in the regions of large-scale production such as the Parisian basin, where the emphasis is almost exclusively on the market, lack the skills necessary to set up farms in the humid zones. Human beings are capable of evolving and of understanding, of course, but an accumulated knowledge has been lost.

Have milk quotas had their day?

Let us begin with a pernicious consequence. When there was a milk surplus in the mid-1970s, powdered milk was stockpiled. It took a ton of crude oil to dry a ton of powdered milk, surely some sort of record in economic folly. By the end of the 1970s, a million tons of powdered milk was crammed into European warehouses, and this was in addition to the stockpile of 900,000 tons of butter. The FNSEA had no wish to challenge the system established by the Pisani laws. The growth of the dairy industry in France had been based entirely on the fact that the taxpayer bore the cost of the consequences of the system. From time to time, when it became necessary to empty the refrigerators crammed with hundreds of thousands of tons of powdered milk and butter, a humanitarian gift was made, to Russia or to some developing country. Given that the producers had already been paid for the milk, and that its storage was subsidized, it was possible to sell cheaply or even give away large quantities of butter (which had sometimes been kept for five years and must have been very close to its use-by date). This had the pernicious effect of encouraging a certain laxity and begging mentality in the receiving countries. Don't bother to support your own agriculture, it said, because every now and again we'll give you fifty or a hundred thousand tons of butter.

Measures that may have been sensible to begin with went on to have pernicious consequences. In the case of the 1984 decision about milk quotas, an aberration was built in.

Towards the end of the 1970s, the watchword in the dairy industry, then totally in the hands of the FNSEA, was: 'Produce as much as you can, and produce faster, before measures are taken.' This advice was not given to all farmers, only to those in the inner circles, well up in the co-operatives, or with access to those in the know. We, for our part, were asking for a quantum system, arguing that not all milk should be paid for at the same rate. The system for supporting the market in milk meant that consumers were paying about 25 centimes per litre without realizing it. Since the price of milk was rising every year, the biggest producers had a strong incentive to maximize production. We were among the minority of farmers who asked for a ceiling to be put on the number of litres of milk according to the number of workers on the farm, with variations according to region. There would be a fixed price for, say, the first 100,000 litres per farm, with no subsidy for milk produced in excess, though farmers would be free to produce more if they wished. If a litre of milk at 1.60 francs was being subsidized to the tune of 25 centimes, included in the price, only 1.35 francs would be paid for additional milk produced. If it was unprofitable to produce more, farmers would restrict their production, but in any case the community would no longer be encouraging farmers to overproduce. That was our proposal.

On 1 April 1984, the Minister of Agriculture, Michel Rocard, decided in favour of quotas. This was a deal struck between the European Union and the FNSEA. On that April morning, the existing state of affairs was frozen, with a reduction of 4 per cent all round. Whether you produced 300,000 or 30,000 litres of milk, the reduction was still 4 per cent. The impact was not the same. For those who were already in a strong position, all was well. For others, it was a disaster, especially for those only just keeping their heads above water; this included farmers who had been unable to expand their production over the years because they had never been in a position to acquire more land, and farmers just setting up, such as the young man who needed to build up his equipment and who was stuck on his father's farm with 60,000 or 70,000 litres of milk. After this freeze, in the second year of the quotas, the general and regional councils, together with the French government and the European Union, financed a restructuring programme aimed at encouraging small producers to abandon their farms and get out of farming.

The FNSEA did not want the quantum, which would have made it possible to adjust production between farmers and between regions. It preferred the quotas. Worse still, when the quotas were decided, it chose not to manage them but to leave the companies in control. These companies had only one aim, to get their hands on the liquid gold to be found on farms – that is, milk. The fate of the small farmers was not their concern. We should remind ourselves that the industrialist of that period did not know the men and women who worked on the farm, his only concern being the market value of their products. The government allowed the entrepreneurs to get rid of the small farmers.

Those in the know manipulated the quotas. This was how it was done between 1984 and 1995. Every year, when farmers had failed to reach their quota, there was milk available. A sort of pooling process was operated between producers, who might be allowed to produce 1 or 2 per cent above their quota. The companies that called the shots warned the big producers three or four months before the end of the year and, thanks to their large herds, they were able to respond immediately as the situation evolved; sometimes they even bought five or ten more cows. The small producers, in contrast, were left in ignorance. 'We have no information; there's nothing we can tell you,' they said. But they warned of the risk of producing even twenty litres too much: 'You'll be paid 1.80 francs for them, but the penalty will be 2.50 francs. It's not in your interests to produce a surplus because you'll be heavily penalized.' The small farmers, trapped in this system, were perplexed. 'What am I supposed to do?' they said. 'I may produce five litres too much, or 100 litres, or 200 litres? How can I tell?' Meanwhile, the biggest producers, those who were well up in the co-operative or close to the industry, were saying: 'I've got 30,000 litres more than my quota; my limit is 300,000 litres a year, but I've been told it's OK.' When it fixed the quotas, the government had failed to establish any administrative system worthy of the name that would have allowed adjustments to be made. Its policy was to eliminate small farmers. The result is that between 1984, when there were still 450,000 dairy farms in France, and 2000, when only 150,000 remained, a space of sixteen years, 300,000 dairy farming families were uprooted (that is, some 540,000 working adults), at public expense, in line with the restructuring plans financed by the general and regional councils. This has been ratified by successive governments, of both the left and the right, which have been happy to see men and women driven off the land. This catalogue of disasters was financed, orchestrated and politically managed, irrespective of party.

Today, nothing has changed. For proof, one need only consult the report of the Office du lait (Onilait), which is jointly managed by the FNSEA and the government, published in mid-January 2001. What does it say? There remain 150,000 milk producers; the restructuring is well under way; the economic and financial pressures are such that, by 2010, only 50 per cent of them will remain. While outwardly deploring this situation, the unions and the dairy industry have nevertheless set a target of 70,000 dairy farms. In the interim, the dairy businesses that are in the bosom of Onilait will do everything necessary to eliminate the small men. This has been planned since 1 February 2001. The French state, which every year, through the intermediary of Onilait, devotes a large sum of money to assisting this restructuring, and the regions, which are responsible for the contracts of the state–region plan, will support them. We urgently need to return to the principle of the quantum to put a stop to this haemorrhaging and to preserve small and medium-sized dairy farms.

France is one of the most wooded countries in Europe. The exploitation of her forests is largely in private hands. While some stretches of woodland are extremely well managed, others never see their owners. Would it be possible to involve farmers more closely in silviculture, which is also of value in regenerating the air we breathe?

The state must recognize that trees and forests play a major role in the great ecosystems, and it is on these grounds that it can intervene. A policy to encourage the management of woodland could be a way of applying pressure on private owners to get them to look after their woods. The state could tax the non-management of private woodland.

In many rural communes the owners of the châteaux used to look after the local forests. The restructuring of farming has led to the absorption of so many small farms into big units that the neighbouring woodland has been put at risk. Farmers have been deprived of all the many uses of wood. In the past it was used to repair fences and to make hoops for barrels, faggots and firewood, and handles for forks, spades and mattocks. A wood was a source of wealth to a farm. The problem is that the whole rural world that valued this inexpensive form of energy and maintained the ecosystem has imploded. We cannot return overnight to a situation where every farm has a coppice or a wood, but the upkeep of woodland ought to be seen as part of the maintenance of the natural balance. The transformation of the countryside by human intervention has to be taken into account. In many regions, the 1 per cent of the budget that is supposed to be devoted to rehabilitating the environment and planting trees has been used to repair church towers. When civil society comes to accept the necessity of keeping its small farmers, or at the very least of protecting its agriculture, it needs to be aware that you will not defend nature by protecting a few songbirds. It is a matter of varied and complex balances.

On the farms that no longer have a wood, might it make sense to offer to manage private plots?

Whatever the type of farming and whatever the region, the reincorporation of woods, coppices and hedgerows is essential if we are to restore the ecosystem for plants, animals and humans, especially in livestock farming areas. Farmers must be involved in this.

Is it reasonable to ask farmers to preserve a certain level of wildlife on their farms? This is not part of a hunting agenda but an expressed aim of the scientists responsible for biodiversity.

The disappearance of human activity throws everything out of balance. In many regions, as soon as there are no more men, women or children, wildlife returns. If settlement and farming are reintroduced, the situation readjusts. A balance can be maintained between fauna, flora and everyday life. When human beings disappear from an area, nature gets the upper hand. This can be a source of conflict. Until now there has been a sort of antagonism, either all one thing or all another; the farmer cleared the land and eliminated predators, while the biologist established totally separate and closed-off reserves. When self-sufficiency was very precarious and there was no regulation, this was understandable. But biodiversity is now endangered. We cannot allow this war between hard-line ecologists and farmer-hunters to continue. It is in the interest of neither side for the antagonism to persist; each party ought to set its own house in order. It is all a matter of balance. Every sort of crop encourages its own particular type of game. Partridges are found in cornfields, hares in apple orchards, and rabbits at the edges of woods. Maize is now grown almost everywhere, and there are plenty of deer but fewer rabbits, hares and partridges. It is not the deer that have chased out the partridges, but an excess of maize and the use of chemicals; the rabbits have nowhere to shelter because the hedges have been destroyed.

If we were to return to diversified farming, every region would rediscover its natural environment. In a populated countryside, self-regulation would operate once again. In practising monoculture and specialization, we have selected the types of game and pleased no one. Peasant farming practices could be a factor helping to restore a balance between the ecologists, who see themselves as saviours, and the hunters, who sometimes want to run the show on their own territory. This guerrilla warfare could become a thing of the past if each party would only put aside their extremism.

We need to get away from a situation where the big landowners dominate the local hunting fraternity. When there are several hunting associations in small communes, relations with the farmers are more relaxed. The area is restocked with game, it is preserved, everyone plays their part, and there is intelligent cohabitation. Unfortunately, this is not universally the case, and where private hunting reserves predominate, conflicts occur. They will not be settled by laws but only by the application of a little common sense, as appropriate to the local terrain, and in a shared respect for the ecosystem. A monopoly is not tenable. Social life has to be put back at the heart of the debate if people are to live in harmony.

10 Have we Learned the Lesson of the Epidemics?

Vaccination against foot-and-mouth disease was stopped for economic rather than for health reasons. The lamb-buying countries did not want vaccinated animals that might be healthy carriers of the virus and might contaminate their own cattle, in America especially.

Vaccination has been stopped; it was expensive both in itself and on account of its non-traceability in meat destined for export. Foot-and-mouth disease is encouraged by the transport of animals debilitated by intensive farming methods.

The recent crisis ought to have been followed by a serious debate in Europe and the wider world about the role of vaccines. Should vaccination be a routine procedure to prevent the disease from spreading? Or should we consider a different approach, that of building up the animals' immunity and making them better able to resist and themselves fight against certain predators or viruses? If livestock rearing was more widely distributed throughout the country and less intensive, and if the animals were fed appropriate fodder crops, they would be much more robust and more able to look after themselves. It is now possible to stop the spread of foot-and-mouth disease without resort to panic measures such as wholesale slaughter, for example, by using essential oils and plant-based products and by strengthening the animals' immunity. The disease could be stamped out, and never again would between 300,000 and 500,000 animals be killed because 150 or 200 were infected.

Those in power acted in the name of the great precautionary principle: 'Better to sacrifice 10,000 animals now than a million later.' The public health officials gave no thought to the psychological trauma so pointlessly inflicted on farmers. At least, during the BSE crisis, the cows were taken away to be killed. The slaughtermen did their job. But during the foot-and-mouth epidemic, the sheep were slaughtered on the spot, leaving the farmer to face not only his empty buildings but also a repugnant and noxious charnel-house in his own farmyard. The sight of so many carcasses on the lunchtime and evening television news disgusted the meat-eating public. From the beginning, horrifying, medieval pictures of funeral pyres appeared on the front pages of English newspapers. People had already been put off beef by all the pictures of carcasses in abattoirs so obligingly shown, even though they were told that it was impossible for meat products to be contaminated. Now it was the turn of lamb, even though there is no risk whatsoever (no transmission to humans). The televised images were quite enough to put viewers off meat altogether. Those responsible had underestimated the impact of this televisual shock treatment.

No serious attempt has been made to identify the profiteers who cashed in on this crisis. These repeated crises are reprehensible, just as organized crime is reprehensible. These 'accidents' do not happen by chance. It is hardly innocuous to send images of burning animals all round the world, nor was it innocuous for the other countries which suffered the consequences of the panic stoked up around BSE. During the outbreak of swine fever in the Netherlands in 1997, 50 per cent of the livestock were slaughtered. In the case of the BSE crisis, it was decided in Europe to destroy whole herds on account of a single sick beast, even though there is no animal-to-animal transmission. The same policy of wholesale slaughter was adopted in the case of foot-and-mouth disease. These political and economic choices kept the wheels of business turning, setting in motion a whole spiral of sales ranging from pharmaceuticals and chemical inputs to feedstuffs for animals. To produce in order to destroy, with the taxpayer footing the bill, appears to be a perfectly acceptable practice in the eyes of the WTO when a health scare looms. If it was a crisis of overproduction and states were asked to pay, we would be told that this was a subsidy on production, and therefore illegal.

Making the taxpayer pay has become a stock response to these repeated crises. Who decided to burn the flocks and herds? Who signed the order for the auto-da-fé? There were those who did very well out of this irrational response to the crisis and the fecklessness of governments and the European commissioners.

It is almost as if these 'accidents' were premeditated, so that the giants of agribusiness, on the other side of the world, would be rubbing their hands and thinking to themselves: 'We'll get the lion's share of the market.' One effect of these crises has been to accelerate the disappearance of a number of small livestock farmers. England spent the equivalent of 100 billion francs in the space of three months on foot-and-mouth disease; the Chancellor of the Exchequer declared: 'Small farmers represent less than 1 per cent of the population; farming produces an annual surplus of no more than 40 billion, whereas tourism brings in 500 billion.' It was implicit that you could no longer give 100 billion francs to fund the wholesale slaughter of livestock when the return was only 40 billion. In other words, we've had enough of farming; in the last analysis, better to let it decline and let small farmers die out. This, in sum, is the analysis of the Chancellor of the Exchequer, with his eye on his accounts.

It goes without saying that the more that small and medium-sized farmers are killed off in the course of these health crises, the more, once the dust has settled, industrial agriculture will expand. A locally based farming will be a thing of the past. That is why it is important for farmers to form an alliance now with consumers in order to revive it.

The citizens of Europe have a different take on things from those elsewhere in the world, such as the United States. In Europe, there is a real awareness of what farming is and ought to be. If we want to break out of this infernal spiral of disappearing farmers and increasing concentration of production, ways of winning the confidence of consumers will have to be found. This can only be done through real transparency with regard to production methods. This is the prime guarantee. We have to be able to demonstrate to purchasers that the animals have been fed in a certain manner, that they are of a particular hardy breed that is less fragile and presents fewer health risks, and that the workers have been operating in certain defined conditions. If we are to promote contacts between the farmer and the consumer, we have to get information about the true costs of production into the public domain. Consumers must demand that the labelling of a product is not confined simply to an indication of provenance. It should also record the minimum production costs all along the line from the farmer to the customer, including the remuneration for the farmer's labour and his social security contributions. People must be made aware of the true cost of the merchandise, that, as things are, a whole series of highly profitable mark-ups are taken at different stages during the processes of manufacture and treatment, and that the farmer is not responsible for all the value lost in the parallel circuits.

We have still not learned the lessons of the mad cow disease crisis. The prohibition of feedstuffs with animal remains in them is not definitive.

The BSE crisis, we are told, is behind us [see Map 6].

At the beginning of the third millennium, in a Europe in which thousands of people are engaged in research, the introduction of rendered animal remains into livestock feeds has had to be stopped because there is no scientific certainty regarding the causes of the infection, the damaged or healthy anatomical parts, or the transmission to humans or other modes of propagation.

Does the prion live in the soil? Do impoverished soils encourage its spread? Which agents are the carriers? Where and when will the prion reappear?

Another question: is the fact that no incident was discovered prior to 1980 because certain procedures had always been observed previously, such as heating feeds with meat in to 133 degrees centigrade, under 3 bars, for 20 minutes? Did the epidemic spread when these precautionary measures were no longer practised?

Another unknown: are all feeds containing animal remains dangerous, or is it a problem of their composition and preparation? Is the use of certain waste materials the real cause of the proliferation of the prion?

The principle of feeding herbivores with feed containing meat seems to be an industrial aberration. Apparently, a director of the Musée de l'Homme, André Langaney, contests this on a priori grounds: 'There is no scientific proof that giving feed containing meat to a ruminant is against nature.' That is all very well, but his observation applies to wild animals, not to livestock bred selectively.

In 1923 Rudolf Steiner, initiator of biodynamic feed, made this prophetic claim: 'To make animals eat the remains of the same animals is a dangerous cannibalism. One day, an animal will show signs of madness.' Nobody took him seriously. Before the age of the computer and hyper-sophisticated technology, we relied on empirical observation of animal behaviour. Today, no researcher is able to answer this simple question: if a cow eats feedstuffs containing the remains of poultry, will the effect be the same as if it eats the remains of animals of its own species?

So, what are we to condemn definitively? Specific cannibalism or any feeds containing meat?

If we assume that the prion lives in the soil, we can hardly begin to heat arable land to 133 degrees; in any case it still survives at 600 degrees.

In France we have abandoned the production of plant proteins. Are we to start producing them again or import them in large quantities?

The old peasant farmers had a set of basic values: respect for the soil, the air, the water, nature and the fauna. In the name of profit and the market, these values have been abandoned. A return to them would be a public health measure.

To close this chapter devoted to the plagues and risks to which all farming is exposed, it might be useful to present a concrete example of what can be done on a farm of 30 hectares, when, as in 2001, a long period of drought was followed by floods and then yet more sunshine. François Dufour describes the experience of one small farmer in the spring of 2001.

Farming seems to suffer far more than in the past from the vagaries of the climate. The planet is in a period of turbulence. We need to draw on past experience when faced with catastrophes of this type.

If leached soils are to be able to absorb the rain and store up water for future crops, there will have to be a return to farming practices that are, sadly, remote from the techniques now employed in certain sectors. The soil has to be broken up with toothed tools and allowed to grass over in the autumn, and the hedgerows have to be restored. The hedge itself serves a number of purposes as far as the flora and fauna are concerned, and also aids water retention. So when, thanks to an anticyclone, a long sunny spell follows a period when the soil has been flooded, what practices are advisable, and how can we compensate for the losses of the impossibility of planting? For field crops, on an organic farm, if the seed has not yet been planted, the first thing to do is to open up the soil in order to aerate it. If a crop is already growing, it must be harvested as soon as it is ready and the soil then opened up so that it can breathe.

The problem is that for many years now, where nature has been forced with irrigation, the soil has been rendered incapable of righting itself between seasons. The more a soil is irrigated, the more irrigation it needs, because it becomes compacted and can no longer breathe. There is no easy way out of this situation. It can only be done by growing crops that will re-create the vegetation, aerate the soil by their roots, and re-create the humus.

What have you done on your farm since the floods?

Already this autumn, we have gone over the land with spring tine harrows, removing all the mosses and the accumulated water and rot round the plants. We raised the small roots of the grass and put compost on the soil just before winter. The compost, as it rots down during the winter, will act as a support, and as a protection for the plants in case of frosts; it will also regenerate them by the slow decomposition taking place between November and March, which will convert the nitrogen and give the first yield of grass. The aim is to feed the grass with organic matter, prevent the soil from freezing, and also to regenerate the meadow for the coming year, restoring its vigour and allowing it to thicken up and recover the oxygen which the excess water had previously been removing. This is of the greatest importance.

In the spring, more work will be done on the meadows; they will be harrowed once again, and gone over with a machine that scatters the molehills and removes all the worm-casts accumulated over the winter, to restore freshness to the plants. Nature will do the rest. But these operations will be carried out with the appropriate tools and without recourse to chemicals. There is no need of chemistry to regenerate plants that have been choked; all that is needed is work on the plant and the soil using the appropriate tools.

What did you plant after the spring floods?

By March the soil had been well prepared and aerated and was ready for the spring cereals; I planted oats, wheat and peas. The machines had gone over the old meadows between February and April. All the moss (and God knows, there is plenty of moss in winter!) had been removed by the harrow, and the plants could breathe in the soil. We spread trace elements that, with the rising of the sap in March, will help make the plants sturdy. These are in my view the most appropriate techniques. They can be used for sowings of beet or fodder crops in early summer – for example, fodder cabbages or rape seed to be eaten in the autumn. If the soil has been choked by weeks of rain, it is ploughed, worked with articulated tools, and frequently turned to warm it up and restore its 'taste for life'.

All this work on the soil illustrates how farming can return to a respect for the biological cycles.

11 Food Follies and the Label Lottery

François Dufour converted his farm to meet organic specifications. But he is not convinced that this is the model for the future or that organic farming can be a universal panacea or miracle cure. He sees it rather as one possible way forward towards the multiform agriculture of the future.

In any case, organic production remains marginal in Europe. In France it accounts for only 0.5 per cent of agricultural production, in Germany, Switzerland and the Scandinavian countries for between 5 and 7 per cent. Just 1 per cent of French farms have gone organic. In Germany, the Green Minister of Agriculture plans to extend organic farming to 20 per cent of farms. France is lagging well behind in this sphere in Europe, importing 70 per cent of the organic products it consumes. Should organic farming in its present form be encouraged, improved or abandoned as outdated?

Organic farming today is an essential element in the reorientation of agriculture and the new choices for its future. The term is used for the products of an agriculture that is subject to a set of very specific requirements and that meets certain criteria. But it is also a symbol for a society that wants to reappropriate its food supply and to eat food that is the product of real skill and traceability. The people who are switching to organic produce are often curious to know what lies behind the label, who, that is, made the product and what methods they used. They are attracted by something that responds to their desire for quality and flavour and that is also low risk.

There are other options that are suited to small farming. For example, the AOC offers a guarantee of geographical identity, that is, of a region or a *terroir*, and the quality marks. It is essential that the term 'organic' is not allowed to become an alibi for continued support for a two-tier agriculture. To accept this would be to endorse the liberalist dogma that creates two types of consumer, one rich and the other poor, the former consuming niche products of high quality, the latter making do with the rest. Segregation along these lines is unacceptable. Every citizen has the right to food of good quality.

The price of organic products ranks them as the food of the privileged, dishes for the elites.

It is hardly the fault of organic farming if high-quality produce is at present accessible only to the rich. The responsibility lies rather with the productivist model, for its failure to take account of all the elements that society needs. Any policy that encourages an emphasis on quality – including organic – deserves to be encouraged; society should demand it. But we need to be careful; organic farming or small farming without people – that is, farming not rooted in a region or an environment – will be equally disastrous, because it is this that gives value to the role of the farmer and all the tasks which farmers are called on to perform. So let us have no organic farming or small-scale farming that does not bring men and women back on to the land.

It is not enough to issue decrees, such as that 20 per cent of farms will be organic by such and such a date. The German Greens, who were once opposed to anything nuclear, are now in favour of anything organic. But organic farming can only ever be part of a bigger picture. In any case, the German Greens are in danger of getting caught in a trap of their own making: East Germany is currently flooding the shops with organic produce that is cheap because it is industrial, that is, it meets organic requirements but is produced without the skilled labour of men and women. Let us not fall into this particular error in France; let us not, that is, erect organic into a religion. We, for our part, see organic farming as part of a multiform agriculture reoriented towards the needs of society.

Organic farming has its limitations. It is usually defined as a method that uses no chemical fertilizers or pesticides, and is therefore more respectful of the environment. But these ecological criteria of organic farming are a handicap in the fight against parasitism: the use of copper as a fungicide is to be prohibited in 2008; the organic seeds that make the most of mineral fertilizers are more vulnerable to disease; organic wine-growers have no weapon against golden Flavescence; how is mastitis to be treated on dairy farms without antibiotics?

Organic farming, like any other sector, will pay the price if it brings no benefits to society. If copper is a danger to health, it should be prohibited now. But at the same time, there should be government research to help farmers who have gone organic – or biodynamic organic – to find solutions to basic problems. After all, the use of antibiotics on cattle is permitted in organic farming twice a year as long as the drugs are prescribed and administered by a vet. We should beware of fundamentalism in all shapes and sizes. Just because, during the thirty years of the growth of intensive agriculture, the watchword was 'anything goes', and nothing was ruled out that could squeeze that little bit extra out of the system, we don't need suddenly to stop using and ban all medication and all new technology.

The good sense of the peasant farmer will see to it that, in the end, not everything is rejected. There are products that can still be used, if in a more restricted and more carefully managed way than during the 'Glorious Years'. The need to consolidate the soil so that orchards and apple trees would need fewer chemicals has often been forgotten. As soon as the farmer begins to see to this and a better balance is achieved, the trees visibly improve.

At the end of the day, organic farming will only have a future if farmers succeed in keeping control of their produce through all the stages of its journey to the consumer. Otherwise, there is a risk that it will be industrialized and therefore perverted. If farmers are confined to the role of producers of low-cost raw materials, the food processing giants will do everything to reap the benefit of the added value and reclaim the margins which the farmer has been able to gain through technical improvements. If, on the other hand, farmers do the processing themselves, thereby holding on to the added value, and insist both on transparency in the matter of production costs and on a guaranteed minimum reward for their labour, the food giants will be excluded, both from the early and the later stages. In which case, the future of organic farming is assured.

If the labelling system revealed the true prices to consumers, they would be clearer about the mark-ups taken by the processing and distributing circuits. The beneficiaries of these circuits reject transparency of production costs, especially in the case of organic farming. The price paid to the organic producer is about 25 per cent more than that paid for the standard product, but when organic produce is offered to the consumer, it can be 100, 200 or even 300 per cent dearer. Let us take the example of a litre of milk: the price paid at the farm gate is 2.5 francs in the case of organic milk, 2.25 francs for conventional milk. In the shops, organic milk is sold for four, eight or even ten times the 2.5 francs received by its producers. It is obvious that enormous mark-ups are being taken all along the line by intermediaries who are exploiting to their own advantage the organic image and the product of the farmer's labour. Quality is poorly rewarded, but the rewards for processing and distribution are lavish. At the end of the day, organic produce comes to be seen as a luxury.

The French quality marks – 'red label' or 'AB' (Agriculture Biologique, that is, organic) – are no guarantee of the raw materials, so it is perfectly possible to avoid chemical fertilizers and use polluted seed – without being aware of it – and still qualify for an organic label.

It is already one of the organic specifications that seed cannot be treated. Since the majority of GM products have antibiotic markers, like certain maizes, it is clear that these seeds cannot at present be used in organic farming, except fraudulently. But organic producers need to be extra vigilant in insisting on a total absence of GMOs and in guaranteeing traceability for their customers. If a producer claims to be organic and allows GMOs in, he or she must immediately stop paying a certifying body to inspect the farm. This brings us back to the question of whether this is food for the rich or food for the poor. Whatever the financial situation of a family or a society, there should be no trifling with people's health or with fundamental principles. It is the job of farming to feed people with high-quality produce in sufficient quantity. To this end, organic produce ought to be given the same level of financial support as other products, that is, there ought to be an overall shift of subsidies from productivist agriculture to quality agriculture. If organic farming expands, the area devoted to large-scale or intensive farming will diminish. A redirection of public subsidies is similarly needed to encourage farmers to grow crops that are appropriate to their soils and to the needs of the market, and to ensure that small farmers are adequately remunerated for their labour.

Organic farming currently receives very little in the way of assistance. The state gives some help to convert over a period of three years. A lump sum is awarded to farmers who are in the process of adapting and who often face a reduction in yields. The subsidy compensates for this handicap. They are then left to depend on the market price of their produce. As a general rule, however, European subsidies are not aimed at high-quality production. The CAP favours the farms that concentrate on producing primary materials.

All the supermarkets now devote some shelf space to organic produce so as to cash in on a current fashion and demonstrate their ecological credentials. But, faced with the organic vegetables sold by smallholders from market stalls, the 'natural' wine, fresh eggs and cheeses sold under a handwritten sign proclaiming '100% organic', and the trendy products called 'organic' but without an organic certificate, you begin to wonder what exactly 'organic' is.

On the supermarket shelf, 'organic' is fashionable. But it is imperative that misleading advertising is stopped. If a product has not obtained proper organic certification, it should be impossible for it to be sold as organic. It is from a concern for authenticity that farmers who are truly organic take the precaution of signing a contract with a certifying body which carries out three or four inspections a year and tests samples of their produce; it can then be sold with an official mark that is a guarantee of pretty draconian controls on its production. In the case of milk, for example, as well as inspections, a sample is taken after every milking, every two days, and tested in a laboratory, which attempts to detect anything that might possibly contaminate the milk in some way. The system is currently well organized.

The United States, too, has its organic labels and organic products that can boast reliable guarantees. Each state has developed its own set of specifications. The producers receive a decent reward for their labour by supplying the local markets. In Europe, each country has its own specifications. An attempt to draw up a single list for Europe as a whole is currently under way. Major tensions have emerged because the scheme threatens to be notably lax and would offer less of a guarantee than is presently the case in France. If we really want to achieve coherence and sustainability in organic products and their sale, the whole of Europe has to adopt the same standards regarding the levels of incorporation of products in animal feed. Organic producers are permitted to buy a minimum of feeds for export to give to their livestock, but these purchases must continue to be firmly restricted without any dispensations. At this level, Europe still has a long way to go.

Organic farming has the value of reminding us of an important truth: yields cannot be standardized, but ought to be adjusted according to the agronomic value of the soil. Let us take the example of a soil whose nature and situation mean that it can produce a yield of 40 quintals of cereals per hectare, although yields on the adjacent land may reach 60 quintals. On the former, when it is producing naturally, given what the soil can provide to the plant, in the best possible conditions, with human labour and natural ingredients such as com-posts, the temptation to exceed the 40 quintals should be resisted. If a product is to be identifiable by a consumer and taste good, nature should not be violated, in organic or any other farming. Organic farming only really makes sense when it restores the relationship between the soil, nature, the micro-climate and an appropriate crop. Unfortunately, people are now converting to organic in sectors and systems that are very little different from industrial farming; they will never provide the real value that the consumer is seeking.

Is it possible, at a pinch, to plant GM seeds and have an organic certificate?

If we do not campaign to get the practice prohibited, it is possible that in certain parts of the world there will be an agriculture that is called organic but uses GMOs. The firms that genetically manipulate seeds have set out to woo farmers who want to obtain organic certification. They tempt them with offers to supply clean seeds that can no longer be attacked by pests, and that are prepared and ready for use. This is light-years away from any agronomic relationship between the soil and the farmer. There is a constant threat from predators who want to control farming in whatever shape or form, including organic. Small farmers must not allow themselves to be cut off from their sources and their roots; they need to think hard about what it means to be a farmer.

It is by no means easy to convert to organic farming. If farmers truly want to change to high-quality production, and not just acquire a logo that says so, they have to proceed gradually. It is a serious error for anyone who works in the food sector to act in response to economic indicators alone. If people have not been prepared or fail to prepare themselves for a change of direction, they can change as often as they like, but their chances of success will be slim. It is perfectly possible to end up switching from industrial productivist agriculture to a pro-duction that may be called more natural but is still in effect industrial. [see Map 4.]

Let us now turn to the question of food myths, a hotchpotch of ignor-ance, prejudice and untruths. Take the example of eggs, about which consumers are understandably perplexed. How are they to choose between free-range eggs, fresh eggs, barn eggs, extra fresh eggs or eggs laid on bars? We are spoiled for choice, yet who is kidding whom? Down with industrial production! François Dufour offers a consumers' guide.

The production of low-price eggs is cast in the same mould as the rearing of industrial chickens in confined spaces. First we need to distinguish the true from the false. Eggs laid on bars, for example, are said to be of better quality than eggs laid on straw, because they are cleaner. This is a claim that should be consigned to the scrap-heap. I was in Rennes recently, at the invitation of a society called 'The University Feast', for a debate. Also present was a very grand chef who works in the Champs-Elysées. At the round table, in front of some 400 young people, I spoke about battery eggs and explained that when hens are reared in a confined space, their eggs are of poor quality. A member of the FNSEA interrupted to say that he would rather eat eggs laid on bars than eggs laid on straw. It was some of the young audience who pointed out that it wasn't the shells he ate. I think he regretted his intervention. The grand chef then said, 'Monsieur, I think you are wrong. Do you, a farmer, really believe that an egg laid on bars is of better quality? What makes an egg are the conditions in which the hen has been reared.' In spite of this, however, there were still some in the audience muttering that, when all is said and done, bars were cleaner than straw.

What gives an egg quality is first and foremost the nature of the feed given to the hen, the type of meal and concentrates. The best-quality eggs are laid by hens that can breathe the fresh air and run around in natural surroundings. The bird develops muscle and a certain richness. In fact, the nutritional quality of an egg is already determined by the time it is conceived.

Another example of fallacious indoctrination is the assertion that food that has not been pasteurized is dangerous. The Codex Alimentarius says that, to avoid all risk, it is better to eat pasteurized cheese; only then can you be sure of not finding bacteria. But nothing can compare with a cheese made from unpasteurized milk. This is an example of the precautionary principle misunderstood and misapplied. There are those who want to put the consumer off anything natural, by insinuating doubts: if a product hasn't been chemically treated, it isn't safe to eat. In fact, precisely the opposite is the case: the natural product, not treated chemically, is less precarious and more stable. In the past, when there were no refrigerators, our parents kept their meat in the meat-safe; pigs were reared over a longer period of time, not intensively, and using natural products; as a result, the fat and the lean would withstand the passage of time simply by being immersed in salt. Today, if you take some industrial pork and try to preserve it, even if you salt it, the meat will start to run, dry out, and quickly reach a condition in which it may actually be poisonous.

If cheese made from unpasteurized milk, which is easy to make and has a good flavour, keeps well, it is because it will normally have been made according to very strict specifications.

We need to rehabilitate all that is natural by affirming that nature knows what she is doing and that a balance needs to be struck; no one should believe that, as we liberate ourselves from machines, we are going to liberate ourselves from the land.

We touch here on the changing life-styles and changing behaviour of the citizen, but also on a system that has brought the increasingly fierce competition of globalization; we touch, in fact, on monopolies. Within the WTO, the Codex Alimentarius is an authority controlled by the FAO and the WHO. Two or three years ago, this Codex attempted to stop all production using unpasteurized milk on the pretext that such products were dangerous. This move is part of a prophylactic campaign being waged on the extremist Scandinavian or American model, an attempt to keep consumers away from anything that might possibly be sullied by human contact.

The time has now come to talk more about good food and less about junk food. Let us emphasize the pleasures of eating and claim an educated palette as a right and a liberty. The indictment of junk food has echoed round the world; it is time to enter the era of builders and cooks.

It is the young, in particular, who should be persuaded to taste good food, rather than forever being lectured to on the subject of what they ought not to eat, and being told that there is too much fat or too much synthetic sugar in the sorts of food that form their staple diet. It would be easy to introduce them to good bread, to real pizza, light and unctuous, and to farm cheeses and specialized dairy products. All the talk about junk food in the year 2000 was certainly useful in provoking discussion within the family and in administering a sort of electrical shock to society as a whole. People are asking more questions, and we can now be confident that good food has a future. The food that is healthy to eat is often the food that is good to eat. And eating well is a way of eating safely.

The more production chains have been rationalized, the more unstable their products have become, so that they have to be freeze-dried from start to finish of the process. It has become clear that the worldwide transport of foodstuffs that are fragile because of their production methods means that the products themselves are highly vulnerable. Industrial poultry has to be frozen within a very short time of leaving the abattoir to stop the meat from going green, as it so quickly begins to turn, even in the slaughtering line. Most current products, however efficiently graded and prettily packaged (twenty-four tomatoes to the pack, all exactly the same size), cannot withstand either fresh air or stress, even less minor knocks, and they cannot be kept. The leftovers, put aside for tomorrow, quickly go off. If you forget to put them in the refrigerator, or if the temperature in the refrigerator is too low (internal thermostats would be a public service), there is a risk of food poisoning from the very products that are supposed to be safe, but which are in reality liable very quickly to become the opposite.

There is great confusion between products packaged fresh, with a use-by date, simply 'fresh', or 'fresh' but defrosted. It is not sufficiently well known that the length of time a perishable item can be kept varies with the method of production. The question is not so much 'is it fresh' as 'is it alive or dead?' François Dufour tells of a little demonstration.

Once, when my refrigerator had broken down, a joint of roast pork and a chicken that had both been started kept perfectly well for almost a week; the meat did not deteriorate, and it was excellent. Of course, neither had been bought pre-sliced or cellophane-wrapped.

I happened to tell a friend about this little experiment in the keeping qualities of traditional products. He told me he had only recently bought an industrial chicken in a supermarket, defrosted it when he got home, but then left it a day before cooking it; a horrible smell then emerged from the oven; it had gone off. He had been sufficiently annoyed to go back to the supermarket, only to be told: 'Yes, with this type of chicken, once it's been defrosted, you have to cook it straightaway.'

A hospital cancer specialist has recently emphasized the dangers of industrial products and praised organic foods. He was responding to the familiar and entirely baseless claim that organic products are much less protected than other highly treated products.

You cannot keep meats from industrial livestock farming as long as the meat from animals reared on a proper farm. The former are atrophied as they have absorbed none of the vitamins provided by daylight, and they lack muscle. These insipid substances are time bombs if not eaten immediately. A corn-fed chicken, by contrast, can be kept for a week; you can eat a little of it each day, and it will still be perfectly OK. In the days when every farmhouse had a ham hanging from the ceiling, the family ate the meat for five or six months, including in the middle of summer, when it was hot and the salt dropped off; they cut a slice or two from time to time and nobody was any the worse.

According to a study carried out by a parasitologist at the University of Washington in Seattle, Mozart died after eating pork chops infected by the larva of the parasite *T spiralis*. (It is worth noting in passing that this specialist had been alerted to the problem of junk food by José Bové's visit to the town for the anti-globalization forum.) Almost two centuries after Mozart, factory farming, health controls and refrigeration have failed to relieve meat-eating citizens of the need to be constantly vigilant and to exercise great care with the pork chops they have for their supper. Freezing and pasteurization provide only very limited guarantees. The irradiation of green vegetables is now a subject of some concern. Some of the salads cut and sold in plastic bags have been exposed to radiation but are described as 'ionized' on the packet; the food industry prefers the latter term, which sounds better than 'irradiated'.

Consumers cannot be too often reminded that packaged salads need to be rinsed, as does all fruit that has been thawed out. But this is hardly enough to remove all the chemical residues embedded in the edible parts. Fruit and vegetables that have been subjected to ionization resemble industrial chicken in that they have to be consumed with the least possible delay. The living matter very quickly goes bad.

Consumers ought to be told that some risks are worth running, others are not. The chief risk is that of food poisoning. But the preservation of taste is another element in the debate. A foodstuff that is stale can be fit to eat but inedible, even though it is not dangerous. Bread offers a symbolic example: a baguette bought in the morning may have gone soft by the evening or be as hard as iron; to be good to eat, it has to be consumed within a couple of hours.

Bread made with organic flour can be kept for a fortnight. The only proviso is that it has to be stored somewhere neither too hot nor too cold. We have to learn to distinguish between foodstuffs that need to be thrown away and those that can be kept. The refrigerator and the freezer can give a false sense of security. They are no guarantee of food safety.

Another issue that is frequently obscured is the presence of GMOs in foodstuffs, especially baby food. How can we be sure that they are totally absent?

The food processing industry, which often has links with the chemical industry, is far from transparent in its practices. Thanks to patent rights and industrial hygiene it is impossible to gain access to the factories. As a result, it is effectively only those in charge of them who know how the work has been done; consumers have to be constantly in pursuit of transparency and demand to be given information. Labels are of little use if the industry has used transgenic methods.

There is an ambiguity in that a tolerance of 1 per cent is permitted. It would be infinitely preferable if a policy of zero tolerance was imposed on processors and distributors. In which case, consumers could demand that the producers of the raw materials, including the farmers and those to whom they are contracted – that is, their association or co-operative – have no truck at any stage with GMOs. We all of us have a duty to exercise our responsibilities; parent associations ought to insist that their municipal authorities or those running the canteens do not permit any GM foods to be used and make sure that everything on the menu is traceable. The best way of getting rid of a product is to impose a total boycott. If there is no longer a market for an item, it will no longer be sold. But try telling working mothers that they ought to stop using baby foods! They would be totally at a loss because they no longer know what to make with the food processor adorning their kitchen.

Is it possible to trace the presence in food of a scary toxic product such as dioxin?

Dioxin can be detected by analysing milk. If its presence is indicated, it shows that it has been absorbed by the cow. Before it entered her milk, the cow must have had it in her body. Where does the dioxin that is so widespread in meadows come from? From the chemical or bacteriological pollution emitted into the atmosphere by unscrupulous companies that do not comply with the accepted standards. Economic considerations take precedence over the collective welfare. But it is the job of local government to see that standards are enforced in all sectors and that the necessary measures are taken to discourage fraud.

In the case of additives, too, we are poorly informed; there has been no really sustained study of the possible consequences of their use.

Additives are increasingly used in foodstuffs, even though recent legislation has removed some of them from the market. But a wide range remains, not only colouring agents but also antibiotics. Everything that is put on the market ought to be licensed, and new legislation is needed on a European and also a world scale. It is the responsibility of the Codex Alimentarius to assess the quality of foodstuffs according to the criteria of the WHO. It ought to draw up a list of essentials so that all countries observe similar standards with regard to the avoidance of certain products. The problem is that the Codex Alimentarius is not a body made up of democratically elected men and women. It is controlled by experts from the multinational firms, in particular the great seed producers, who exercise a very strong adverse influence on the capacity to develop types of product that would be less dependent on chemicals. This amorphous grouping is badly in need of reform.

It may be utopian to hope for the total abolition of additives, but it would be perfectly possible to eliminate some that serve no useful purpose other than increasing the sales of the chemicals concerned. We could do without colouring agents and preservatives. In any case, intelligibility should be improved without delay. It would then be up to the consumer to choose the products most clearly indicated as lacking in additives. By means of practices that bypass international regulations, businesses are currently using such products to re-create by chemical processes drinks that are alcoholic to varying degrees. It is the responsibility of the Codex Alimentarius or the WHO to enact strict rules regulating the use of these products.

Sugary products that contain animal fats are causing obesity among the young, who eat a lot of them. They have become accustomed to the taste of these sweet things, which are easy to eat, but no one tells them what they contain.

Until recently, it was usual for families to sit round a table and eat a balanced meal, that is, a meal with a starter, a main course and a pudding. At the risk of indulging in wishful thinking, the convivial meal eaten sitting round a table seems likely to survive, along with the reconstruction of a multiform agriculture. In this age of fast food consumed all round the clock, people are eating, without really thinking about it, all sorts of foods that are full of sugar or fat, and that are bad for their health. They are substitutes for meals and appetite suppressors. What they are really eating is advertising budgets. To counter this, there could be information points and commercials telling people how to prepare balanced meals and when and how often they should be eaten. Fast food made with local produce is beginning to gain ground. Freshly made sandwiches are competing with plastic-wrapped pastries.

There has been a tendency recently to play down criticism of certain products, and also antibiotics and GMOs; it has even been claimed that there is nothing wrong with nitrates.

A vet recently called the Confédération Paysanne claiming to represent a group of experts who believe that nitrates in water present no danger to health. 'Nitrate in itself is healthy,' he said. 'It appears that people who drink water containing nitrates all their lives have far fewer health problems.' But how much nitrate? This piece of disinformation is not without echoes of the soothing communiqués issued by the French Atomic Energy Authority whenever there is a radiation scare, along the lines of: 'We are nowhere near the doses which natural radiation is constantly sending through the human body.'

The shock-horror discourse surrounding food, like that surrounding the economy, is already out of date. Doomsday scenarios do little to take us forward. It is a great pity when old fears are reawakened by the encouragement of a psychosis in the name of the precautionary principle; but it is equally unfortunate when the food lobby irresponsibly anaesthetizes public opinion by getting scientists to 'demystify' and 'downplay' every criticism of chemical additives, irradiation, biotechnology and even toxic effluents.

There are people who deplore what they see as a general loss of flavour in organic and non-organic food alike, and even claim that chemical agriculture is no more insipid than any other.

It is well known that once you stop using varieties that have been developed according to the nature of the soil, it is difficult to retain the flavour. Over the years, the old varieties and the old seeds have been abandoned. Harvest by harvest, little by little, the taste has disappeared. Vine-growers have cottoned on to this. The wine industry was at one stage badly hit by the large-scale import from various countries of basic wines intended simply to make up the hectolitre. The producers of fine wines realized that it was not in their interests to join the rush for quantity, and have instead concentrated on identifiable tastes. It would be possible to do the same in the case of most vegetables, that is, to select plants with an eye to their flavour and their nutritional qualities.

With something of the same idea in mind, the French *boulangerie* has transformed its image through the diversity of its breads, at a time when the reputation of its baguettes had sunk pretty low. Bakers have returned to the old yeasts, flours and methods and campaigned for greater traceability on behalf of consumers.

As a result, both bread and wine have benefited from a new image and from the determination of skilled producers to retain consumer confidence by offering a range of attractive and agreeable products with a good flavour. People are recovering their taste for bread and wine.

Taste is also dependent on temperature. Food that is systematically chilled on health grounds can lose its flavour and become insipid.

Where products are alive, they should not be stored in the same conditions as pasteurized dairy products. A quality cheese, made on the farm, using traditional methods in strictly controlled conditions, will mature beautifully if it is kept somewhere cool, but do exactly the opposite if it is frozen. The taste comes from the refinement of the cheese in a cool place. If it is put in a refrigerator, it turns into a sort of putty.

The situation is similar in the case of meat. It has to rest, and it needs to be kept somewhere cool, protected from the sun and from heat. It should not be consumed immediately after the animal is slaughtered. It should be left to rest for at least four or five days before it is cut up and offered for sale. Today, too much assembly-line meat has spent no more than a dozen hours in a refrigerator before it is sold. Most meat now leaves the abattoir within a few hours of slaughter. But when an animal has taken four or five years to become adult, the flesh needs at least a week after slaughter to develop its full quality and acquire its full taste.

People often think that if a cow has given milk for three or four years, its meat will be tough because of the animal's age. But if the meat is left in the fridge to rest, in the proper way, for a week or so, virtually no difference in terms of sweetness or mellowness is detectable compared with the meat of a much younger animal that has not put on fat. The debate is based on false premises. People think that cows that have given milk are no longer good for meat. In the current climate of mistrust, they are likely to tell the butcher, when shopping for beef, that they want meat from a bull of a good breed, not a milking cow. They are afraid that if it is a cow it may have been given animal feed containing meat. But this is sheer prejudice. The reality is quite the opposite. It is true that the meat will not be of the quality of Salers or Charolais beef from an animal that has spent four years out at grass, but if a bull or a milking cow has been reared naturally, their flesh will taste very similar. Everything depends on the type of feed the animal has consumed, also on the length of time between slaughter and consumption. When a cow has been lactating, it should not be slaughtered at once but left for six or eight weeks after the last milking so that the beast recovers its firm flesh.

Today, fruit is kept out of children's sight. The familiar fruit bowl ornamenting the middle of the table has disappeared. Instead, everything is kept in a compartment at the bottom of the fridge; the fruit itself is rarely seen, brought out only at the last moment.

For a fruit to develop all its sugars and all its nutritional properties, it has to be kept at the ambient temperature, but protected from damp. If, with the aid of chemistry, it has been brought on in the shortest possible time to become a semblance of a fruit, it will be tasteless. In the case of industrial tomatoes, a certain number of days after being planted – if we can still call it 'planted' – the fruit are picked and sent to the factory where they are made into concentrate. The process bears little or no resemblance to real farming. In fact, the 'intensive' tomato no longer needs a plant connected to the soil to grow. What now happens in Holland, England and certain French farms in the department of Bouches-du-Rhône, or what is happening in the Almeria region of Spain, is truly scandalous. In the Almeria, in thousands of hectares of glasshouses, using a heavily exploited Moroccan labour force, the production of industrial tomatoes stuffed full of chemicals has been rationalized to the nth degree. It could hardly be more artificial, unless, that is, the tomatoes were manufactured in a factory or a simple molecule produced a tomato shape.

The growing of other fruits – for example, peaches – is similarly specialized. In the Bouches-du-Rhône, at Saint-Martin-du-Crau, a single producer may have 1,300 hectares planted with a single variety of peach – in which case, he will supply around 13 per cent of the French market. This is a version of factory farming, completely industrialized and quite alien to peasant farming.

Pears are another disaster area. Production has been rationalized as far as possible by standardizing a few varieties with good keeping qualities, and, with the aid of a lot of chemistry, the fruit is kept in the cold for long periods of time. There is no reason why cold should not be used as a way of preserving fruit, but the purpose here is to be able to sell the fruit irrespective of season; we have reached a point where people no longer know what time of year it is, since pears are available all year round. With the genetic manipulation of fruit, it will soon be possible to produce strawberries that ripen at Christmas. It has already been announced that a fish gene will be added to prevent them from freezing. It is now possible to eat anything, at any time of year, in any part of the world, but the food will be tasteless and without relation to nature, the seasons or the sun. It is the ultimate fatuity of the productivist system carried to its logical extreme.

In jars of baby food, quite unrelated flavours are combined – for example, meat and apple. Mothers fail to realize that in return for a very relative gain in terms of time saved they are risking a very serious distortion of their baby's taste-buds. To make a soup with a potato, a carrot, and a scrap of parsnip takes only a few minutes. And the baby's menu can be varied daily, with other fresh vegetables, or an egg. The first taste the child learns to know is that of its mother's milk. The quality of this nutritious liquid is linked to the type of food the mother eats, so her milk changes from one day to the next. If she continues this education in simple flavours by means of food she makes herself, she will be able to observe the gradual emergence of an appreciation of taste that becomes an essential part of the person as they reach adolescence and eventually adulthood. It is a mistake to pander to children's likes and dislikes and abandon the attempt to introduce them to a range of tastes. When they reach the age of reason, they are at liberty to choose for themselves, but there is no substitute for an early education in the subtlety of flavours if they are to use their freedom wisely.

12 Landowners, Farmers and Managers: Who Owns the Land?

The question in the title implies two others. The first is legal: does whoever owns the land exploit it? The second is social: how easy is it for someone who wants to become a farmer to acquire or rent land? There is also a third, and politically dangerous, question: who, without having rights in the land, appropriates its wealth?

To find our way through this labyrinth, we need to distinguish between title-deed and mandate to manage. Who controls the farms? It is not, as in the past, the local lord of the manor. The age of the landed gentry is long over; they no longer have the financial clout.

Control is external, distant and invisible; it is in the hands of the lending institutions, those who run the CAP, and those who reap the benefits – that is, the directors of the food processing firms listed on the stock market.

The way the land is used is now more important than the way it is owned. And the way it is used is determined by the nature of the production systems imposed by the decisions of agricultural policy-makers or the lobbies.

The key issues are access to land and the transmissibility of the farm. There is a legal, social and political battle to be fought, and on the result depends the revival of sustainable agriculture.

When there is a succession and the son or daughter wants to take over the family farm, what obstacles have to be overcome? And what are the chances of young people from outside who want to go into farming?

It has become very difficult to take over a farm because of the accumulation of capital. There remains, however, one fixed point: the fundamental rights over the status of the tenancy and over management and transmission. This is absolutely crucial. Increasingly, however, we are seeing more intense competition between farmers already in possession and young people anxious to establish themselves and take over the family farm or another available farm. This is the first element in the problem.

The second is the lack of short-term profitability when a farm is first taken over, which means that young people are often unable to get a viable project off the ground due to economic and market constraints. They lose the credibility with the banks needed to get a loan or security, especially if they opt for production without added value. One solution would be to provide opportunities for young people to start farming on small units that needed only limited investment – since we inhabit a world made precarious by the economic system – and establish themselves with a value-added product that could be offered for sale in local markets. This is one way in which they could be enabled to make a start.

With 50,000 people leaving farming every year, the deficit is dramatic. It raises the question of opening up the career to young people from outside, since the number of farmers who come from farming families will continue to decline.

About 10,000 farms are taken on by newcomers every year, of which fewer than 6,000 receive official support. Those who have the money, a training and no need to borrow are in a tiny minority. The majority are without a qualification and choose to farm outside the production norms, adopting progressive methods. These are not deemed 'professional' start-ups. These beginnings of a repopulation of the countryside and revival of rural life are certainly to be encouraged. It remains necessary for the structures to be adapted to reality, since reality is not going to return to the norms. It is obvious that things are going to change. The problem is how to encourage the trend so that the number of new farms is not in deficit. It is a tragedy that farms are disappearing, and that people who want to set up as farmers, when land becomes free, are often obliged to make do with the leftovers, while the best lands are snapped up by those who are already well provided for. Ideally, there would be no barrier between those who lived in and off the countryside and the professional farmers. It ought to be possible, when new residents put down roots, for their children to be able to become the new farmers.

The number of children from farming families able to take over farms is not enough to sustain the number of small enterprises at the current level. We need to prepare for the arrival of people from outside. Such an opening up of farming would bring about a revolution. The farming of tomorrow, if we manage to retain a reasonable number of small farms, will be differently composed. It will develop many more links and opportunities for exchanges between town and country. Ideally, it would not be necessary for young people to have to buy land. That is why we need to find formulas for land associations such as the Groupements Fonciers Agricoles (land associations) in which local communities could invest over a period of years.

In the Larzac, once the plan to extend the military camp had been abandoned, the state granted a long lease of agricultural land to a specially established company, the Société Civile des Terres du Larzac (SCTL).

In France, the Larzac is the most significant example of renting by state concession (6,300 hectares). A few small GFAs exist elsewhere, which have taken out options in a number of regions, but they are not very extensive. The management of land in the Larzac through the SCTL was a 'first'; the land still belongs to the state, but it is managed by a society which has a long lease renewable after sixty years and settles all legal aspects directly with the local farmers; it also applied the regulations while respecting ways and customs, in particular regarding the protection of the soil and its ultimate purpose. It is a special case, since its first task was to bring back into use for arable and livestock farming land that had been doomed to desertification. This contract serves as a useful model, since it avoids the need for the farmer to buy the land at each generation. The inheritance system for landed property in France is absurd. How can farmers achieve economic coherence if, at every generation, they have to bear the cost of land transfers? Where land is privatized, forms of GFA could still be developed that would enable a group to buy shares in land and make it available to a farmer within a specific framework. We need to make use of the Farmers Statute in its present form while also developing ways of protecting property and its proper use. The notion of land as public property is still not sufficiently widespread.

The dominance of the capitalist system in agriculture has challenged the very basis of the use of the land. The rush to acquire slurry-spreading rights is so intense that agricultural or food production is no longer the point; the sole aim is to profit from spreading slurry. The land has changed its nature and is no longer ours. In highly speculative sectors like pig or poultry production the land itself often belongs to the banks.

This brings us to the need for a redefinition of rural areas. The concept of land ownership is a given, but another concept is beginning to emerge: the use of the land belongs to us all, and we all share responsibility for its upkeep and exploitation. If we do not challenge the notion of private property, the idea of a common heritage, or common asset, can appear paradoxical and be a source of conflict.

The Napoleonic Code says that private property is inalienable. The owner of an asset can do more or less what they want with it, as long as they do not break the law. Today, this poses a fundamental problem. If we consider agriculture in relation to its mode of production, the environment and future development, the landowner cannot operate in isolation, and so the use of the land concerns other people too. First, there is more than one way in which land can be used: it can be a production tool, a hunting ground or a place for gathering mushrooms, among many other things. We need, therefore, to think about ways of managing land use that are disconnected from private ownership. Such a separation exists in the case of hunting; in France, local hunting associations are typically responsible for the management of one type of use: the farmer has the right to hunt, but the owner can grant the hunting rights to an association that has responsibility for a specified area. In the communes where all hunting is managed independently of private properties, collective rights take precedence over individual rights.

There is no reason why something similar could not be made to work in agriculture. It is perfectly possible to envisage a situation where the agricultural use of the land is determined at the level of the commune or canton, especially now that it is quite common for a farm to have several owners.

José Bové and his associates farm land as a Groupement Agricole d'Exploitation en Commun, or agricultural co-operative, with eight different owners. The link between these owners is their farm. If one of them one day decided not to relet to them but to let to someone else, the farm, therefore, could disappear. But if the commune, canton or department were to draw up a plan stating that it was necessary to maintain a certain number of farms in a certain area, the owners would remain owners of their property, but the duty to let the land to keep farms in existence would become a legal obligation. A system of penalties in case of non-observance, or failure to rent out, could be instituted, the crucial factor being the declaration that the continuation of the farm was in the public interest. It would not be depriving the owners of their rights; it would simply be to maintain farms in accord with a superior right, based on the need to plan rural development and to make land available for farming, subsidiary services and other activities such as hunting, rambling and country holidays. It would be to recognize land use as a common property of the community, not something that can be reserved for the enjoyment of the proprietors alone, or even for the activity of farming alone. The fact that someone works a farm does not give them *carte blanche* to do whatever they want with it; they are operating within a context and an environment that must be maintained for future generations.

We ought to be thinking about a new social contract for the use of the land. The person given responsibility for working the land would not necessarily be its owner but would guarantee that the fundamental mission of the land would not be distorted in a speculative manner. This would be to reappropriate the role of the peasant farmer not as owner but as promoter of life.

This approach could be extended to all the legal aspects of the rights to produce and rights to subsidies. At present, several people are involved: there is the person who owns the title-deeds and who has a supervisory right; there is the working farmer; and there is the policy-maker, through whom a right to subsidies (when the land meets the criteria for support from the public purse) has been superimposed on the rights of the owner and of the working farmer, but within a legal framework that is undefined. Land became highly desirable once the political decision was made to inject 2,400 or 2,500 francs per hectare. Brussels grants irrigation subsidies in certain sectors, but has never sorted out the question of the subsoil or the groundwater. When Europe encourages irrigation by subsidizing it, who then 'owns' the water in the subsoil? It hardly belongs to the community, when, from one day to the next, it can be drained or polluted by a single individual. All the wealth that lies underground ought to remain the property of the community and not simply of whoever is farming in a certain spot. But responsibilities with regard to the water, the air and the soil are not yet officially recognized in the Declaration of Human Rights. It should be supplemented by a Declaration of Duties towards Nature.

Rich countries and industrialized countries anxious to hang on to their internationally competitive edge over other countries are now even talking about the right to pollute. They say, for example, to poor countries: if you have no ores to exploit, and because your land is poor, let us at least buy rights to pollute in your countries, and we will stockpile our surpluses and waste materials there. We should not ignore the 'rights of the soil' and all the multifarious ways in which human activities interconnect at the level of the subsoil. The people who are proposing to bury nuclear waste for millions of years have no idea what the consequences might be for the living world constituted by the subsoil. The soil has 'rights', as does the subsoil.

Can the citizens who live within the Espace Schengen choose to move to France and farm there?

Within Europe, people are now free to move and settle wherever they choose.

But for people from outside the Espace Schengen, for example the Slovaks or the Kosovans who want to settle in France, the situation is very different. How can we speed up rural repopulation?

Illegal settlements are made on poor land or on plots of doubtful legal status. Those who come from countries within the European Community settle in areas where there is already great pressure on the land. If they own land at home, they can sell it and buy an area four times as great in France. If they get as far as Spain, they can buy eight or ten times as much land. There is no level playing field. Foreigners settle by acquiring land. But the Kosovans and Bosnians who move into the French countryside do not have enough money to set up a farm. This is another reason for making a clear distinction between land ownership and land use, and for instituting a leasehold status for the new arrivals. In any case, renting is now commonplace: nearly 60 per cent of French farms are rented as opposed to owned outright. If you have to buy land in order to work it, you are obliged to increase production in order to pay off the purchase costs. This is totally counterproductive. The only people to gain from the process are the bankers who lend the money. It is in no one's interest that farms have to be bought in full ownership. At the European level, it generates increased production that serves no useful purpose and is subsidized to no good end. It deprives others of the possibility of living off their farm without being obliged to repay the loans to buy the property. It would be a great boost to resettlement if it was made possible for income to be used to support families rather than to reimburse the Crédit Agricole.

Could job-creation schemes be established in farming? When Martine Aubry was at the Ministry of Work and Employment, such schemes applied primarily to security work, for example in educational institutions, but not to jobs in the countryside.

It is important that people who live in the country are not cut off from the rest of society by their living conditions. For some years now, groups of employers have formed small associations to recruit an employee whose time and costs they share, a little in the logic of the Coopératives d'Utilisation de Materiels Agricoles, which purchase agricultural equipment for the shared use of their members. More could be done in this field, as in Norway during the 1960s, when there was a deliberate policy of support for small farmers in order to improve their conditions of life. A system was devised to provide 'substitutes' to enable farmers to take a holiday. Every farmer had the right to a replacement for three weeks or a month in the year. If the provision of substitutes was regarded as a social right for farmers, on a par with paid leave for wage-earners, it would be perfectly possible to create jobs that would be collectively administered. At the same time, young people from outside farming would be provided with an opportunity to spend two, three or four years preparing themselves to take over a farm at a future date.

Employment opportunities in the country are further reduced by the increasing concentration of landownership. In the current system, there is nothing to stop a farm being dismantled when a farmer retires and the land being absorbed into a larger and expanding concern. The principal buildings are often resold to people seeking second homes, to help offset the cost of the purchase. Even if some of the land becomes available later, it is no longer possible to re-create a farm because there is no farmhouse.

In many rural communities the sheer number of second homes and holiday cottages alters the balance of activities and also the balance of political power, as the farmers often end up in a tiny minority. Some municipal councils are run by residents whose votes can influence the way the village functions, even to the point of excluding any farming activity from the village itself. Nature becomes a leisure complex rather than an area of mixed use in which agriculture is combined with rural tourism. If we break the social tie in which the countryside is both agriculturally productive and a location for leisure activities, we are encouraging a situation in which intensive agriculture, like heavy industry, is completely cut off from the areas devoted to tourism: on the one hand, silos, on the other, theme parks, two worlds that never meet.

It would be possible, when a farm is to be surrendered, for there to be a pre-emption in favour of anyone who wanted to keep it as a working concern, so that they were given priority over a purchaser wanting the house as a second home. For this, we need a declaration that start-ups and employment in agriculture are of public utility, and also legislation giving priority to start-ups over expansion and dismantling. As a preliminary, we need a Farming Register that would decide what farms are. A first step would be to change the policy of the SAFERs. Originally, it was the purpose of these societies to exercise a pre-emption on agricultural land in order to let it to farmers. Thanks to the malign influence of the FNSEA, leases began to go to cronies and various shady characters. A society that aimed to impose limits on enlargement and gave priority to the installation of new farmers would be more useful. Owners who did not wish to rent out land or who preferred to dismantle a farm would have to pay a heavy tax because they would not be operating within the guidelines of what might be called 'land councils' run by municipalities or cantons. Unfortunately, a few years ago, SAFER changed its statutes. It no longer has an obligation to sell land on for farming; it can sell to whoever it wants, which these days usually means an estate agent.

What would happen if, starting tomorrow, all farms below a certain size were designated as conservation areas?

The Code in its present form contains no definition of a farm. We can define, more or less, an agricultural worker, the livestock, and the relationship with the owner, but there is no precise legal framework for the farm itself. The Modernization Laws made provision for a Register of Farming that was supposed to list the farms in each *département* and the resident work force. This Register exists in theory but has never been put to use. It is the Chambers of Agriculture that are supposed to administer them. They have preferred that the whole issue should be kept obscure, for fear it might lead to a declaration that farms ought to be re-leasable with rights to produce. In the 1990s the

departure of the oldest farmers was actively encouraged by the introduction of the 'structured early retirement' option. What a dreadful
expression! A farmer had the right to retire early if he found a neighbour who would take over his land. But the farmers who were owners
often remained in their buildings because they had nowhere else to
go, or they sold their farms as second homes so that they could buy
somewhere smaller or move in with their children. The result was a
disastrous increase in the number of farms dismantled and the near-
impossibility of young people getting hold of a farm.

On what criteria should such a register be compiled?

The first step would be to describe the farm, and how it is worked,
directly or indirectly. The farm is an area of land, with a group of farm
buildings, which establishes a physical link with the soil. On these are
based the right to produce that is linked to this particular farm and
that should not be transferable. Farms are enlarged because quotas are
linked to surface area; the way to increase your quota is to acquire
more land. Once the farm has been defined, it should be the turn of
the work force. Finally, at the departmental level, a geographical map
could be drawn up and a decision made as to the level of rural activity
to be maintained in terms of a given number of jobs and their distribution throughout the *département*.

13 No to Rampant Globalization

José Bové, when was the first time you specifically said 'no' to globalization, that is, when did you first realize that, by a sort of chain reaction, what happens in one country has repercussions in other countries? When did you first become aware that there is an international dimension to the question of small farming, and that a farmer caught up in the productivist system may indirectly contribute, without wishing it or realizing it, to the poverty and ruin of farming in distant countries?

It all began with the incorporation of agriculture into the General Agreement on Tariffs and Trade during the Uruguay Round of 1986.

The first time I fought against this North–South logic, however, was much earlier. It was in 1974, when we organized a rally in Larzac on the theme of 'corn gives life, weapons kill'. We argued as follows: as long as agricultural land in France is being taken over for the testing of armaments destined to be sold to countries in the South, the purchasers will obviously not be spending their money on developing their own agriculture. This seemed to us all wrong. More than 100,000 people, including peasant farmers from Africa and Latin America, attended the rally. During one of the debates, on the pernicious role of our industrial agriculture, especially at the level of off-soil farming, the logic of soya imports was attacked. It was then, through the question of soya, that I began to appreciate the perversity of a system which effectively dooms entire regions of the planet to be producers of raw materials to feed the animals that we, in Europe, keep off-soil in sheds, especially in the west of France, Holland and Denmark; and that our farming is effectively based on the use of the best lands in the southern hemisphere to make it possible to rear livestock that are then sold back to these countries at low prices. Even before people began to talk about globalization, I had come to realize, along with my friends and correspondents, that our European mode of production was based on the exploitation of countries in the South, whether South America, Asia or Africa. That was the starting point for my battle.

Today, as much as 16 million hectares of land is devoted to the production of soya to be imported into Europe. In the southern countries, an area equivalent to half the cultivable land in France is employed to produce food for our livestock. It is a system that beggars belief. The growth of our animals is being accelerated thanks to the end-product of the exploitation of whole regions in other countries. This sort of agricultural production no longer has any connection with the land. It might just as well be done in cities, on concrete floors. We have cut the tie between farming and the land.

This perverse system has been cynically developed by the food processing industry, supported by the cereal lobbies. The factory farming of chickens is expanded in order to maximize the use of cereals, and soya becomes necessary as a complement. Production on this model inevitably demands cheap imports of vegetable proteins. We have destroyed whole equilibriums and re-exported the by-products to the countries of the South. It was not even necessary to have GATT or, in due course, the WTO, for this wholesale destruction to begin. The system was structured and is now rationalized to serve as a model of how production should be organized throughout the planet.

In 1986, when agriculture was integrated into GATT, the current orthodoxy was for tariff systems between states to be organized so as to prevent the market from becoming a jungle. The original idea was not bad in itself. Unfortunately, by a distortion of this logic, the concept of organizing the market was replaced by a sort of dogma that holds the market itself to be a factor for good. It postulates that the more market-oriented we become, the more growth we create, and the more growth we create, the more development will follow. From this has emerged a discourse of free-market utopianism: 'Thanks to the opening of frontiers, we will create a free market, and this free market will of itself bring prosperity.' GATT embraced wholesale this angelic free-trading ideology, and it was decided to include agriculture in the international agreements so that it would be integrated into the market at all levels.

At the time of the first meeting of GATT, early in 1986, small farmers knew very little about this multilateral international tool. The average citizen did not see it as likely to have any effect on the realities of daily life. In the 1990s, at the end of the Uruguay Round, it became clear that there had been a shift in the relationship between states and the economy, and that the latter was now operating in an increasingly autonomous fashion. The transnational companies had their own logic, and often wielded significantly more financial clout than did states. They were able to influence the multilateral negotiations in their own interests, assisted by the fact that the governments of the rich countries let themselves be persuaded that free trade was the only possible form of international organization in the commercial sphere.

It was in 1998 that the OECD produced its plan for a Multilateral Agreement on Investment. For the first time, it was stated in a document, in black and white, that 'in consequence of this agreement, a company may take legal action against a country for impeding its expansion'. For the social movements, this was a terrible shock. It was brought home to them in no uncertain manner that this logic was in the process of changing the relationship between political power and the power of big business; the companies could bypass any national legislation, concerning the right to work or any other right, saying: 'Your legislation is incompatible with our expansion; it must be changed.' Under pressure from the social actors, France was one of the first countries in the OECD to take a step back and declare that it could not sign this text. This sparked the first global awareness.

In 1999, the McDonald's affair in Millau was the second major event to send out an alarm signal and mobilize public opinion. It was made very plain that even public health was subject to the laws of the market. The WTO had first criticized Europe for refusing to import hormone-treated beef from the United States and Canada, and then declared illegal the erection of barriers to prevent the entry of such produce on health grounds; this action came as a revelation to many people. Things came to a head when the United States was authorized to impose surcharges on certain European products, including Roquefort cheese. This most venerable French speciality was being held to ransom for the purposes of commercial retaliation. This concrete act and this powerful image made it blindingly obvious to the general public that the law of the market was not simply an abstract game played between companies, but something that adversely affected their daily life. The repercussions were enormous.

The recent dispute in South Africa over access to Aids drugs has been another great jolt to public awareness. The South African government had set in place the provision of generic drugs, including triple-drug therapy, to treat those suffering from Aids, at a very low cost. Forty-seven laboratories and the United States lodged a complaint against South Africa before the WTO for theft of patents. The same thing happened in Brazil. The general public perceived these actions, too, as an assault by the market on public health. In the name of the right of companies to protect the patents on their drugs, millions of Aids victims were to be doomed. This rampant commercial logic, which obeys only the laws of the market, has subverted the hierarchy of values between human and commercial rights.

What has brought together the so-called anti-globalization movement is the assertion that the market is not a value in itself; its organization can potentially be a regulatory tool, but when fundamental rights are ignored, it becomes a perversion. Once this is realized, the necessity of organizing the planet on the basis of a different set of values becomes apparent. This extends far beyond agriculture, but since agriculture is at the heart of life, the debate about the ways in which it has been perverted and alienated gives us a clear vision of the future of the planet.

Agriculture is an essential starting point for the organization of life and of trade. It is a sort of litmus paper for any observer of the mechanisms by which society is regulated. Many African countries now import huge quantities of wheat, in particular from Europe, and the traditional modes of production are being abandoned. The urban population is growing in Africa, as elsewhere, and it is easier to supply it with bread made with the flour from one of the great flour mills that have sprouted in the big African ports; this wheat flour is replacing sorghum and millet. Local farmers receive some support to make their bread half of wheat and half of local produce such as millet, but such projects are doomed to failure because the home-grown products are dearer than the imported wheat. They make their bread, accordingly, wholly of the latter. The system has been completely skewed. This is why the question of food sovereignty, the right of peoples to be allowed to provide their own food by means of their own farming, is a fundamental right. If it is denied, the planet has no future.

A country that produces rice must import a minimum of at least 5 per cent of its rice consumption, and the same applies to other products. This obligation to open frontiers to the big United States and European transnationals enables them effectively to dump their cereals, because their production costs are much lower than those of the receiving countries. This rapidly destroys the capacity of poor countries to produce their own food, making them dependent on food produced elsewhere.

The productivist system itself is wholly indefensible. Those who accuse us of fighting a rearguard action are already well aware that their cause is lost as far as public opinion is concerned. The model can no longer be justified, and there is no one now prepared to defend it. Its former supporters accept that the process must be changed. It is doomed always to be chasing its own tail. Its days are numbered. What would happen, one wonders, if it were to be put on trial before a court, for example in Stockholm? The best tactic available to the defence lawyers would be to oppose one ideology to another, and argue, in the hope of impressing the public, that anti-globalization is an ideology that is anti-liberal. But there is no ideology in the rising tide of public opinion, simply a wish to survive and to defend the resources and heritage of the planet, and also people's lives.

The transnationals are stealing our vocabulary. In the name of special interests they speak of free trade or the free market, whereas what they have actually done is increasingly privatize markets to the exclusive benefit of the great monopolies. The word 'freedom' has been hijacked. 'Globalization' was to begin with a humanist concept of encounters, of ways of enabling people from all over the world to have connections with each other, to trade, and to travel from one place to another. It is one of our ideas. We all live on the same planet, and we all have interests in common. It is we who are the true internationalists.

José Bové remembers having been a conscientious objector, in contact with other recalcitrants from many parts of the globe. Later, he joined the ranks of those who style themselves 'citizens of the world'.

Our awareness dates from the aftermaths of two world wars. When countries have fought each other, it has often been on behalf of the economic interests of a minority whose only aim was to make money – for example, the steel cartel. There were people who said: 'No, we will no longer fight on our frontiers; that sort of logic is dangerous – we are citizens of the world.' The 'globalization' movement was initially humanist in inspiration. But the word has been corrupted by those who, in the name of free trade, have reduced 'globalization' to opportunities for the free circulation of their goods without any restrictions and all over the world, so that the logic of the market will become the logic that incarnates the world. Words like 'freedom' and 'sharing' have been stolen. The logic has been turned on its head; it is now we who are accused of being 'anti-global'.

There has been talk of the end of ideologies with the end of dictator-ships, and the death of totalitarianism has been acclaimed. But forced technocratic globalization appears to be taking over where totalitarian-ism left off.

A significant example is the behaviour of the peasantry when Poland was subjected to the Communist yoke in 1944. The collectivization of land met strong resistance in the countryside; the Soviet model of the *kolkhoz*, the state farm, did not work in Poland, which retained a large number of small farms, including market gardens, dairy farms and pig farms. What Communism failed to achieve in forty years, the European market will achieve in ten. The integration of Poland into the European and international markets will destroy Polish agri-culture a good deal more rapidly. The peasants may have resisted Communism, but they are finding it very difficult to oppose the law of the market. In this way, we are up against a dictatorship in fact if not in name.

The same phenomenon is found in China, but on a different scale; the entry of this country into the WTO threatens an eventual massive rural exodus of 200 million peasants.

The cartel's most recent achievement in their assault on our vocabu-lary is the word 'modernity'. What is true modernity? Is it to vilify small farmers for refusing to make use of the latest techniques and most recent discoveries and for trying to stifle research? Or is it to refuse to give in to a scientistic ideology? To wish for an ethical dimension and a level of moderation and control is a very different thing.

In the eighteenth century, to be progressive was to want to make it pos-sible for people to live a better life, and to want culture, material comfort and liberty to be accessible to all. What happened to this word during the course of the twentieth century is nothing short of astound-ing; the idea of progress as human betterment was abandoned, and it was given a purely technological logic. Progress is now the name given to what is in effect no more than technological development. Every time there is a technological improvement, we are told 'this is progress'. The improvement of technology for its own sake has become an end in itself. We, for our part, reject this particular illusion of 'progress'.

14 If All the Peasant Farmers in the World . . .

José Bové has travelled all over the world supporting peasant initiatives, studying local agriculture, listening to citizen movements, comparing experiences, and participating in social forums. Conscious of the international dimension of the farming question, he draws attention to the causes and consequences, in the most distant countries, of the crises now affecting the farming community in Europe. The problem cannot be solved at the local level, but only globally, at the international level. His visits to Bangalore, Porto Alegre, Mexico, Seattle and Montreal have made the small farmers of the world feel less isolated from each other.

In Bangalore, in southern India, I attended the 'seed trials' which were then beginning. Some companies had sold sterile seeds to peasant farmers. The witnesses called to testify moved me to tears; women whose husbands had committed suicide revealed the extent of the distress of peasants driven to desperation by the impossibility of coping with the collapse of market prices and the excessive cost of seed. They had even been cheated over the quality of the seeds. Men showed the scars where they had sold a kidney so that they could afford to buy seed. The trial was also an indictment of the pressures bearing down on the peasantry, the burden of the caste system, and the exorbitant cost of dowries at every marriage, which means they are permanently in debt. But the greatest obstacle to their survival comes from the nonsensical deregulation of prices and from the agricultural policy being pursued by the Indian government, which spell ruin for small farms.

India is self-sufficient in milk. I was astounded, therefore, to learn that this great country now imports subsidized milk from Europe; it is cheaper when it arrives in India than locally produced milk. I was shocked by the evidence of the victims, but I also saw that they did not accept that all was lost. Some of them had organized in self-defence, accumulating their own resources, and setting up alter-native models. They were experimenting with seed banks. India pro-duces enough food to supply its population and is not threatened by famine. All the agricultural land is occupied, and the countryside is densely populated. Its economic policy risks driving people off the land. They will only go to swell the population of the shanty towns, and the overpopulation will be catastrophic. I saw reason for hope in the fierce battle being fought in India to maintain and develop the rural movement.

Gandhi's great intuition at the time of independence was his state-ment that the Indian republic would be built on the basis of its villages and not its towns. On the east coast, in the 1960s, a major battle was fought to force the big landowners to grant their lands *en évidage*. Many millions of hectares of agricultural land have been recovered for small producers as a result. We ought to pay attention to the rural movement in India. In this huge country the size of the task is over-whelming, but the courage and inventiveness at the local level are exemplary, and the aims of these peasant farmers of the south and east of the Indian subcontinent are similar to our own.

At Porto Alegre, I arrived at a crucial stage in the battle against GM crops. The Brazilian federal state was not respecting the law of one of its member states, Rio Grande do Sul, which is exemplary in the way it has chosen to defend peasant agriculture and refused to give in to the pressure of a lobby.

In Brazil, there has been no official pronouncement at federal level on the use of GMOs. Rio Grande do Sul, the most southerly state in the country, has quite specifically prohibited the growing of GM crops, including experimentally. Almost unbelievably, in this state, which is one of the main producers of Brazilian soya, private companies ignore the legislation. Monsanto, to mention no names, bought a farm and began to grow transgenic crops on 400 hectares of land; the intention was to produce quantities of seed ready for the day when the battle was won at federal level. This was a wholly unacceptable flouting of the law. The state of Rio Grande do Sul blocked all the seeds, and the company was unable to get them away, but it continued to grow the crops quite openly, as if nothing had happened. Faced with this show of strength, the Brazilian Landless Movement, which now numbers some 10 million people, went into action, having very firmly come down on the side of peasant farming and against GMOs. It adopted the tactic of a land occupation with the intention of being able to legalize the occupation and settle people on the land on a permanent basis. There are a number of projects for alternative agricultures, including the introduction of organic farming and quality marks for the produce. Those who want to promote food self-sufficiency in Brazil as a whole are anxious to show that the defence of high-quality agriculture is not incompatible with the production of sufficient food for those who are now excluded. The overall additional costs of pro-ductivism prove this *a contrario*: producing something of high quality is no more expensive than producing rubbish. An attempt to demon-strate the truth of this on the ground is perfectly realistic and is in no way a rejection of progress.

Near Porto Alegre, I visited a group of farms created by 'legalized occupations'. Of the 100 families settled there, thirty-five have joined together in a co-operative, the remaining sixty-five working their farms independently. No single model has been imposed on the pretext that they ought to work together because they had occupied the land at the same time. On the contrary, each family can choose whether to operate individually or collectively, and the two ways of working can cohabit; there may even be mutual aid between the two groups. The experiment is in itself of great social interest. Also, the production methods, in both livestock and arable farming, are inven-tive. The introduction of organic rice farming and the development of aquaculture to fertilize the rice fields with fish waste are intelligent initiatives. Aqua-feeding by the algae and destruction by the fish of whatever might generate parasites, together with the use of the excre-ment to provide nitrogenous supplements for the rice fields, adds up to a cycle that sustains a sort of complementarity and allows a farm to be less dependent in the early stages and therefore viable. The produce is sold in local markets at prices that are compatible with local living standards. It is an example of how successful farming can be when a social movement is involved and when it is the peasants themselves who construct their model instead of accepting a schema imposed from on high.

This project was organized in collaboration with agronomists. It is important for experts to participate in these experiments, but not to impose anything. Here, the people themselves made the decisions. What is happening at Porto Alegre is a source of hope and also another contribution to the struggle of peasant movements all over the world. When peasants reclaim their own future in one part of the world, peas-ants in other countries should be made aware of it. A sense of a com-munity is innate in rural peoples.

In Mexico, the march with Subcomandante Marcos took place under a human rights banner, but the peasant cause was very definitely not absent. Indigenous communities represent scarcely 10 per cent of the population of Mexico and are often banished to the poorest areas. Chiapas is one of these extremely difficult zones, and home to some indigenous farming communities. Their organized movement of rebellion is called 'Zapatista' – it is they who chose the name – and it fights for recognition of the rights of the indigenous peoples. Curiously, Mexico accords no specific status to the descendants of the first inhabitants of this country, who were massacred at the time of colonization. They are fighting for dignity and for recognition of the specific right of the indigenous peoples to be able to organize themselves, according to their own rules, on the lands they inhabit. They are not seeking autonomy and have no wish to withdraw from Mexico, but they want to be regarded as full citizens. 'Mexico cannot survive without us.' At the same time, this battle is clearly part of the globalization debate. It is not by chance that it started on 1 January 1994, the official beginning of the North American Free Trade Agreement. The insurrection of the Zapatista Movement was launched on the very day of this triumph for free trade. It was to make the point that indigenous people's basic rights are now ignored. The only things to be globalized are the economic and financial interests that are becoming the principle on which the world is organized. The choice of date was therefore symbolic. It was to show that the commercialization of the world actually runs counter to the recognition of the basic rights of individuals and communities. From the beginning the movement was part of a global debate about what is now happening. By calling themselves the 'Armed Zapatista Movement of National Liberation', they deliberately evoked the name of Zapata, the most symbolic leader of the Mexican Revolution, who, at the very heart of this revolution, was above all the representative of the peasant movement.

Marcos himself has an urban background, but in the Mexican Zapatista Movement it is he who truly incarnates the rural Republic. The greatest achievement of Zapata and his movement in the state of Morelos, near Mexico, at the beginning of the twentieth century, was to put in place the 'Ayala plan' of agrarian and land reform. The concept of the allocation of land and its distribution according to use rather than ownership is found everywhere. During the Estates General, on the eve of the French Revolution of 1789, as can be seen in the *cahiers de doléances*, the peasants never fought to acquire land but rather to retain collective use of it within their communes. These are the remarkably constant themes of historical peasant movements. When the native peoples of Mexico chose to evoke Zapata, it was to indicate that their organization extended to include the whole of the rural movement. During the march held in March 2001, what was important was this link-up between the Zapatistas and all peasant movements. We have had contacts with the Mexican peasant organizations since 1985. Representatives of their peasant unions attended one of our first rallies that year, and we already knew that one of the demands of the Mexican peasant movement was the implementation of a new agrarian reform, seventy years after that of Zapata. The march stopped in the village that was the birthplace of the champion of the peons.

Marcos visited the house, which has been turned into a little museum, and this was the only time on the march that the subcomandante and other leaders removed their hoods, as a mark of respect for the founder of the movement; they then symbolically signed the Ayala plan for agrarian reform that Zapata had put in place so long ago. The day after our arrival in Mexico there was a meeting with the peasant movements to discuss the battle against the multinational companies that are currently seeking to impose GMOs. Links between peasant movements and indigenous movements are now found all over Latin America, in Colombia, Ecuador, Chile and also Brazil, where there is support for the movements of the Amazon Indians.

It is not only the Confédération Paysanne, which has supported the Zapatista Movement from the beginning, but a growing number of other associations in Europe that have taken note of this link-up. Citizens are increasingly coming to realize that what is happening locally, under their noses, and what is happening far away, at the international level, have a common denominator, and that policies today are no longer decided in Paris or Brussels. This is what we wanted to demonstrate at Millau in front of the site of the new McDonald's. Roquefort is a tiny corner of the world, at the very back of beyond. The decision to block imports of the local product, with its long tradition, was supranational. The turning point came when it began to dawn on people that even producers with an AOC could, one fine day, find themselves threatened by a diktat emanating from the other side of the Atlantic. Right at the beginning of the struggle, in 1973, a delegation from the aboriginal nations of North America, on their way to Geneva to meet the permanent Commissioner on Human Rights of the United Nations, had come all the way to the Larzac plateau to assure us that our struggle was just. Some of us remembered this, and it was amazing to find, thirty years on, the situation reversed; this time it was we who were in a position to offer them our support.

Life in the country fosters real ties of solidarity. They existed in the past, but our forefathers lived them rather than talked about them. The Algerian war put these ties to the test. If ever you have time to talk to them, the now long-retired peasant farmers who were conscripted into the French army will tell you of their painful experiences in the Algerian countryside, and of their distress at the role they were called on to play in relation to other peasant farmers. In the Larzac struggle, many felt the need to make common cause; perhaps this was in memory of the Kabyle shepherds of the Aurès, who should never have had to confront recruits taken away from their own countryside to fight what was a war in all but name. What had then been left unsaid, at a time when it was believed that the ties between the world's peasant farmers could be broken, resurfaced on the Larzac plateau.

How can solidarity towards the Kabyles be demonstrated?

In the war of independence, the Kabyles paid a heavy price. They have subsequently been spurned by the FLN, who seized power. This original people managed to maintain a communal life after the Arab colonization, and therefore to preserve their culture and modes of organization. But since the revolution they have faced a highly vertical state that has implemented a radical programme of land reform, creating state farms and a system not based on the capacities for self-government of rural communities. It has imposed a sort of agriculture on the Soviet model. In the face of the increasing rigidity of this system, which is failing, the Berbers are now in revolt. The role of the army is unclear. Certain massacres may have been organized to further the special interests of those in positions of power. The seizures of land suggest collusion. Will the popular uprising in Kabyilia spread? No one can tell how things will turn out. But this situation of deadlock cannot continue decade after decade. The system is collapsing and will eventually implode.

Similarly, in the Middle East, the exclusion of the Palestinians is a tragedy. When the state of Israel was created in 1948 peasant farmers were expelled from their lands and villages. Today, acres and acres of olive trees are being grubbed up. First the trees are cut down, then trenches are dug round villages to prevent their inhabitants from leaving.

During his stay in Canada, José Bové made contact with the first nation's people.

I went to Canada twice in six months, first in November 2000, and then again in April 2001. On my first visit I met delegates of the Hatikameq Indians, who live about a hundred kilometres north of Montreal in quite intolerable conditions. The Canadian constitution may grant them theoretical recognition, but their standard of living is steadily deteriorating, and their acculturation is nothing short of tragic. Their lands are being eroded, deforestation continues, and their traditional way of life is increasingly being destroyed. Inside the reserves, people are condemned to live on charity, unable to organize their lives in ways of their own choosing.

When I returned to Canada in the spring of 2001, it was for the Summit of the Americas, or rather *against* the Summit, which was a gathering of thirty-four countries, not including Cuba, which had not been invited. The indigenous peoples from Canada, North America and South America also met, and their rally, in front of the wall that had been built to protect the Summit, had great symbolic power. They asked to attend the discussions in their capacity as the original populations of these lands: 'You are talking about our territories without our having the right to speak and without even inviting us. We do not recognize your boundaries; our territories are different.' They were driven away and were unable to participate. The Summit of the Peoples was a counter-summit with exemplary protocol; each delegation asked to be received by the first nation's people of the Quebec region, the Hurons, and it was they who welcomed them. It was a lesson in democracy for the official summit, meeting behind its barricades.

I did not meet the Inuit. I am not sure whether the word 'peasant' should be used for all the peoples who lead lives dependent on nature. The Inuit are hunters. It remains the case that, whatever the climatic zone and the natural surroundings, every population ought to be able to maintain its own practices and find ways of developing them in the area in which it lives. We feel solidarity with the Inuit because their rights are not being properly protected against attacks on and dangerous intrusions into their space — for example, by the offshore oil companies or the pollution of Thule by the American strategic base near which a B52 carrying four nuclear bombs crashed in 1968. Respect for peoples ought also to imply respect for their environment and for their own forms of development.

In New Caledonia, I met the Kanak peoples. They are engaged in a number of interesting projects that they are managing themselves, on the lands to which they have access in the islands and the northern province. They are preserving both their culture and their traditional way of life, and by exploiting local mineral resources they are taking control of their own economy and reinvesting according to collective agreements.

The situation of the Maohi, by contrast, is critical. The infrastructures necessary for the Pacific nuclear test site were on such a huge scale that people were taken from all the islands to serve as labourers on the atolls of Mururoa and Fangatofa. In due course, these temporary workers were laid off. Today, they are crammed into the shanty towns of the main island of Tahiti, while many islands of the archipelago have been denuded of their inhabitants. The primitive peoples of these places have been completely abandoned and are now living in the most abject poverty. Such are the terrible consequences of the forms of development forced on them.

Tourism is helping to make a bad situation worse. A big hotel has been built close to Papeete on religious sites. Some families lodged complaints. The case went before the International Court of Human Rights, which condemned France for 'violation of the rights of peoples'. But international law does not stipulate that the French state can be forced to destroy the cause of the offence. The illegally constructed hotel continues to prosper, in contempt of what is held most dear among the native peoples, their own beliefs. The Australian aborigines have similarly had to defend certain sacred places profaned in the bush country.

In 1995, when nuclear testing was resumed, a spontaneous revolt by the Polynesians followed the first test. To them it constituted a sort of violation of the sea. As the army had opted for what it called 'transparency', people watched as, on every television screen, the centre of the atoll shuddered; they saw this as an act of aggression against the founding sea of Polynesia, a direct assault on themselves. A sort of Intifada went on for two days, at which I was present as an observer. The Tahitians poured out of the shanty towns in their thousands, attacking anything that represented authority – that is, the airport and the large stores. I will never forget this great outpouring of feeling. Back home in France, all the media comment emphasized 'the violence of the Polynesian', which I found deeply shocking. Institutional violence is never seen as the initial violence; the act of despair is a response to violence, a counter-violence.

The end of the 1960s saw the publication of Archbishop Helder Camara's *The Spiral of Violence*, a wonderful little book in which he argues that rebellion in the face of an iniquitous situation, alienation or exclusion is not comparable to institutional violence. It is legitimate, since legality is impossible. You cannot condemn people who rebel when they are suffering an intolerable injustice. Legitimate revolt is not an act of villainy like the original violence.

My support for the Palestinian people is not a distraction from the cause of peasant farmers. On the contrary, globalization operates in war and in peace, as wars and peace are made or unmade by those in power. Wherever political violence or state terrorism deprives peasants of their land, or prevents them from irrigating their plots by confiscating their source of water, I am bound to offer a helping hand. And the farmers of the Larzac, whose right to farm is not contested, but who are victims of economic violence, market forces and the profit motive, stand together with the excluded and expropriated peasants of the Middle East.

When a people is prevented by unequal power relations from ensuring its own survival, and when their food sovereignty is alienated because they can no longer produce anything, even engage in subsistence farming, the battle has no frontiers.

15 The Weapons of the Peaceful Citizen

A Texan organic beef farmer, a grower of non-transgenic maize and soya, a wild-salmon fisherman from Alaska, and a peasant farmer from the Larzac who wanted to persuade Americans to taste Roquefort cheese: the image of these four men standing shoulder to shoulder spread all over the United States. It was in this company that José Bové was able to make the point that there was no hostility between the small farmers of America and those of Europe, and that they were in agreement regarding a type of farming that would not be industrial. Bové was responding to an initiative by an association of farmers anxious to show that the United States had its high-quality products.

In the United States, consumers are accustomed to the flavour of 'blue-cheese' sauces. 'Blue cheese' is an ersatz form of Roquefort. When they were given the real thing, the image of Roquefort itself was transformed. This traditional – one might almost say archaic – French product became overnight a symbol of the resistance of local farming to standardization, and hence a weapon in a war. For the cheese itself, it was a shot in the arm. The Americans who ate authentic Roquefort felt that they were doing far more than simply eating a cheese; they were striking a blow for their independence. They were enjoying the freedom to choose the sort of food they ate.

This very public tasting was for me a way of thumbing my nose at an American administration which had put a surcharge on imports of this French cheese. I had managed to import a piece of it free by sending it to myself. It was treated as a gift, and therefore taxable, but a 100 per cent tax on nothing was still nothing. Far better than a lengthy speech, this symbolic act denounced the arbitrary nature of the reprisals decreed by the federal administration, making a fiscal hostage of a farm cheese from a country which had refused to import hormone-treated beef.

Archive images of the demonstrations by farmers who have taken to the streets in protest against dumping, falling prices and surpluses have been used and abused by television news programmes. Viewers are shocked when they see cartloads of fruit and vegetables being tipped out and dumped on the public highway. It seems a pointless waste and an indecent profligacy when whole populations in the Fourth World go hungry and an impoverished minority in the rich countries is dependent on soup kitchens. Why throw these surpluses around instead of distributing them?

The sight of food being destroyed is deeply shocking. There is an element of irresponsibility on the part of the demonstrators, people whose work has been devalued and who have lost contact with the reality of the true farming life. Behind these outbursts, however, lurk the men who have done well. They spur on their troops and exploit the despair of hard-pressed small farmers so that they can reap the benefits in the form of increased aid. This, as we have already observed, never reaches the worst-off.

If we look back over ten years, we know to within roughly half a per cent the quantity of a particular product that is needed from one year to the next on the internal and the international markets.

It is not enough to grow just any old crop. We need a land register, along the lines of those of trees or vines in the AOC areas. Yields can be predicted. Those who are determined to put large quantities on the market at all costs are not satisfied with producing what society really needs. Within the European Union, if we cannot establish quotas by country, we need at least to establish Organisations Communes des Marchés (OCMs: collective marketing organizations) that would make possible a rough estimate of demand. The problem at present is that there is nothing concrete that makes it possible to do this. Subsidies are being granted to encourage the cultivation of fruit and vegetables while policies for retrenchment are simultaneously being put in place.

There are those within the food industry who are not in favour of controlling these parameters and who oppose the creation of a regulatory tool. In many countries people are exploiting the system of public subsidies and have no wish for demand to be matched to supply. They make a Machiavellian calculation: 'When we have produced large quantities, we will depress the price paid to the small farmer and then destroy the surplus. We will try to negotiate price support to plug the gaps.'

What is to be done? The fruit- and vegetable-growing business should be reorganized on the basis of an OCM and production should be geared to real need by abandoning the rush to export that generates the surpluses.

The role of humanitarian aid should be included in the regulation of the market. The food processing industry should not be allowed to get away with claiming the alibi of charity, that is, with giving away surpluses once in a while so that it can go on producing them with impunity.

We condemn the institutional violence that consists in a concealed assault on liberties and imprescriptible rights of the citizen, and the commercialization of life. But rather than meet violence with violence, we prefer to mobilize public opinion by acts of symbolic significance; and we aim to make maximum impact by participating in counter-demonstrations, with a democratic debate, peaceful land occupations, and mutual support networks.

José Bové is convinced that new forms of action could be tried.

Civil disobedience   To get the date of CAP reform brought forward, citizens who remember that they are taxpayers have a legitimate means of pressure: withholding payment of the amount they calculate as their tax contribution to the sum that France pays over to Brussels by placing it in a blocked account; it would not be a refusal to pay, but a desire to separate out from one's tax the forced contribution to the CAP, so as to exert pressure for a reform to be agreed before 2006. This sort of initiative is one of the tools of civil disobedience. We resorted to it thirty years ago in the Larzac. We urged people to hold back 3 per cent of their taxes, explaining that this portion corresponded, within the armed forces budget, to the money spent on enlarging the military camps. It was symbolic, but we asked people to send the money to the Larzac to finance the construction of a sheep house. Those who paid this money automatically were prosecuted for tax refusal, because the citizen does not have the right to decide where their direct taxes go. But every trial brought new publicity and swelled our ranks. It is an important and appropriate way of exerting pressure; it can be related to our explicit request for a thoroughgoing examination, under the aegis of the European Parliament, of the condition of farming since the Berlin Accords of 1999. We would like this report to be compiled under the control of the European deputies, with referral to the various parliaments of the debates held by the relevant organizations in each country, with a view to agreeing the reform by 2003. Halfway to the due date, it is high time we got going.

How far is the ballot box an effective way of exerting pressure?   In March 2002, at the Salon d'Agriculture, the candidates in the presidential elections were queuing up to appear on the trade union stands. It was an opportunity for us to test the importance of the small farming vote. Was it a sufficient means of pressure, a strong enough argument to convince French politicians to make a stand, by pinning them down on the question of advancing the timetable for CAP reform, the negotiations about subsidies, OCMs, and changes to the newly introduced Contrat Territorial d'Exploitation (Contract for land use), which benefit those farms that are already advantaged? We asked our visitors very explicitly if they would make a firm commitment, and what action they would take. We pointed out that if they evaded the issue, we could ask people not to vote for those candidates who did not support us at the presidential and subsequent general elections.

The candidates gave every appearance of listening carefully to the small-farming voice, but all we actually got were vague promises and soothing words along the lines of 'I hear what you say' or 'I am in favour of a balanced French agriculture'. They thought they could get away with repeating in chorus that everything necessary had been done to protect food safety and the quality of local products. With the FNSEA in favour of maintaining the *status quo*, they were reluctant to run the risk of finding themselves disqualified at the next elections. The reform of the CAP is a vital issue in national politics, but all we got were slogans that offended no one, without a commitment to reform.

It was made pretty clear to us that we would have to find other weapons with which to continue the battle; we would have to resort to more effective action like the refusal of taxes, which has concrete and permanent consequences extending beyond the electoral calendar.

What lesson should we draw from the last Salon d'Agriculture?   What struck me most was how cut off from the realities of rural life our politicians increasingly are; all they see are the showcases and smoke-screens of agribusiness. The general public, in contrast, is showing increasing interest in these realities and in the protection of jobs, in order to ensure high-quality produce. The day is perhaps not too far off when we will open a Salon for the Small Farmer and Consumer. Direct contact between farmers and the population at large – what a weapon that could be!

We have waited in vain for a formal statement from the French government regarding the negotiations that took place in mid-November 2001 in Qatar, under the aegis of the World Trade Organization. We have not forgotten that the reforms of the CAP in 1992 and 1999 conformed to the rules laid down by the WTO. Today, the CAP is simply the reflection of this organization's demands at the international level. This raises a number of questions: are our politicians ready to begin to stand up to the WTO on agricultural matters, or not? Are they ready to state that the internal policy of Europe is none of the WTO's business, that the vital interests of the European population are matters that will be debated within Europe, and that the WTO is no longer going to dictate our agricultural policy? To do so would be to reject the spiral of dumping and export subsidies.

Recourse to the law   We have submitted a file to the Minister of Justice listing the companies that have bought and sold cattle feeds containing rendered animal remains in contravention of French law. No action has been taken. To appeal to the law against cheats and polluters is to act lawfully, but our experience reveals very clearly the extent to which the rights of the citizen are confronted by a two-speed justice. If a McDonald's is dismantled or a field of transgenic colza destroyed, the law moves swiftly to prosecute and sentence those responsible, even imposing prison terms. But it remains almost totally inert in the case of those responsible for a catastrophic situation in livestock farming and a potentially catastrophic situation in the sphere of public health. The paradox is more than hypocritical; it is cynical. In 1996, we were forced to go to the lengths of stealing customs documents so that we were able to put into the public domain evidence that 132 companies had imported animal feeds from Great Britain, though they had received no dispensations to do this since 1990–1. To denounce such a serious violation, we delivered the file to the office of the Minister of Justice in December 2000. He cannot therefore plead ignorance.

What has happened to the complaint we lodged in the spring of 1996 at the office of Judge Pétillon in Nantes? Union activists in the customs who inspected lorries recorded the movement of goods without the least intention of stopping the trade in animal feedstuffs. Companies that have grown rich on the basis of these dangerous products are now, paradoxically, growing richer still; even if they are doing less well out of cattle farming, the increased demand for chicken and pork means that they are selling a lot more pig and poultry feed. They win on all counts and are not a penny the worse off; in fact their profits only grow.

We therefore lodged a complaint; all the customs documents were at the judge's disposal; the Minister of Agriculture knew what was happening. The case has still not been brought; it may even be said to have been aborted. How, realistically, today, can irregularities in 1996 be proved, or malpractice in companies traced, when feeds containing animal remains are now strictly forbidden. The law cracks down not on the fraudsters but on those who engage in legitimate acts of revolt in the face of situations in which the public interest is threatened. Parliamentary reports were drawn up, but no prosecutions followed, as if those responsible for these crises enjoyed *de facto* protection. Such people are never held to account. It is the consumers, as they buy their meat, who have to pay for the testing for BSE. It is the Minister of Justice who needs to be told in no uncertain terms by the Ministers of Health and of the Environment that 'the polluter should pay'.

Squatting on cultivable land   The illegal occupation of unclaimed land with the sole intention of farming it legitimately has emerged as a form of action that may gain public support. In April 2002 we helped a shepherd and his wife to settle on the Larzac plateau in the very spot where his great-grandfather had been a sharecropper. With the support of union officials, local politicians and neighbours, the squat served as a model of how the right to work the land can be recognized. When other avenues have been exhausted and the situation is dead-locked, an occupation, bypassing the prior need to buy the land, ends the stalemate and makes it possible to keep a farm going.

Would it be possible to make GM crop experiments rebound on those conducting them? For example, when a field trial of transgenic plants is known to be taking place, rather than resort to the tactic of destroying the crop, why not start legal proceedings against the testers on the grounds of the potential risk to which the population is exposed?

The problem is that these trials are now carried out in a tightly controlled legal context, because authorization to grow the crops is given by the Commission du Génie Biomoléculaire (Commission for Biomolecular Engineering). It would at some stage be possible to lodge a complaint, but we all know how slowly these things move. By the time the location of an experiment with transgenic crops becomes known, the situation is already urgent. It is by no means easy to locate the precise sites, because when a trial is to be conducted in a commune, the mayor is informed of the company and the type of trial, but the number of the plot of land and the name of the owner are in a sealed envelope whose contents he has no right to reveal. Public information cannot circulate, in the name of the protection of public health. The legislation is absurd, and judges know the law but nothing else. Friends of the Earth brought a case alleging denial of the citizen's freedom of information, demanding that the names of the communes where trials were being conducted should be made known, and they won their case. This might become a precedent, in which case we could start proceedings immediately a field trial of transgenic crops became known, and it would no longer be necessary to take last-minute action, on the ground, to limit the risk of pollution. But French law being what it is, it is quite possible that the judges would still say: 'As long as there is no law on potential risk, we do not consider there to be a problem' [see Map 7].

In Great Britain, the law operates differently. Cases of this type are heard before juries drawn from the general public. In 2000, fifteen or sixteen Greenpeace militants were prosecuted for destroying a field trial; the majority verdict of the jurors was that the destruction of a trial, including on private property, was not an offence so long as there was a potential risk either to the community as a whole or to the surrounding fields. It was the pressure of civil society represented by such juries that made it possible to decide that the public interest took precedence over the individual interest of the landowner who had agreed to the experiment. On 8 November 2000, for the first time in France, a court in Auch did not accept wholesale the claims of the pro-GM party; it sentenced the protesters who had pulled up some transgenic maize to no more than a suspended 3,000 franc fine, with 1 franc damages to the firm of Monsanto. The company has not dared to appeal. We have to fight our battles with whatever weapons are available to get field trials prohibited.

Mobilizing the consumer   Associations and groups play a crucial role in bringing consumer and producer together. They are experimenting with long-term initiatives that involve making free choices. The impact of the occasional boycott is much more limited.

The 'Fair Trade' organization, for example, which has a network of some 700,000 families, is a grass-roots initiative. It emerged from an earlier experiment in ethical trading, and it consists of paying a fair price for the fruit of the labour of small producers in poor countries. It takes into account the added value of an artisanal product that is absolutely vital to the continued existence of these farmers. When you buy a Fair Trade product such as coffee in a supermarket, you are helping to support these small producers; this is not an act of charity but an exercise of consumer choice. The Fair Trade networks are working for the future. They are in the process of banding together, with a Free Trade Charter, not only in France but also at the European and international levels. They represent a real step forward in the drive to create a different market system, beginning with agricultural production.

Their first immediate effect is to ensure that the labour of the farmers is remunerated and their production costs covered in full. The peasants who produce coffee for these networks receive a price that is 40 per cent higher than the world price for coffee.

The second, less immediate, effect is to encourage production rooted in a locality. The peasants who band together in a co-operative may receive an advance payment on the sale of their produce. It is not simply a matter of their being promised a higher price and left to get on with it; the payment on account gives them a guarantee of income which puts them in a better position to organize and invest.

Thirdly, there is a desire to enable as many peasants as possible in the regions concerned to participate in the scheme. The organization tries not to operate in such a way as to create privileged niches for a few at the expense of others in the vicinity. The initiative is not confined to the act of buying in shops. The work done on the ground in the areas of production promotes local sustainable development. By buying something they need, consumers are helping to ensure a balance in distant countries and provide a livelihood for whole families. From being passive customers they become active agents, influencing a social process by the way they shop.

A link is developing between fair trade in the produce of Southern countries, especially coffee, and the farmer-producers of our temperate zones. The same consumers buy Max Havelaar 'socially responsible' coffee, on the one hand, and farm produce from European peasant networks on the other. They understand the trade-off between a high-quality product and the remuneration of peasant labour, whether in the South or the North. Negotiations are under way to extend the networks to other produce, such as tea, bananas and some other fruits. The range is widening and distributors are being made to face up to their responsibilities. It is not only through what you buy that you can express your solidarity; you can also threaten the shop that does not stock Fair Trade products that you will take your business elsewhere if they fail to provide them within a given period of time. This type of action complements ethical trading in the textiles and ready-made clothing that are manufactured in workshops that use child labour, pay less than the minimum wage, or prohibit trade unions. One can envisage a system of 'ethical labels'. In France this approach is beginning to be applied to high-quality products threatened with disappearance.

Under the label 'The Gardens of Cockaigne', experimental market gardening ventures are being started up in the outer suburbs; families pay an agreed sum of money in advance every month and receive in return a box of vegetables delivered directly to their door every week. Such a system makes it possible to finance the creation of market gardens using organic methods that provide jobs for the socially excluded. The income is devoted to enabling people to reintegrate into society and find gainful employment. It is an initiative that brings together an economic vision, a vision of quality, and a social vision linked to job provision.

In Quebec, there is a sizeable scheme of a similar type aimed at the rehabilitation of small farms; it is called 'Equi Terre', a nice phrase with its echoes of 'equity'. It puts several hundred small market gardeners into direct contact with hundreds of families living in Quebec.

Such experiments are not confined solely to North–South relations, but to North–North relations, too.

In Piedmont, there is a foundation based in an old monastery that is dedicated to encouraging the transmission of culinary traditions. It is called 'Slow Food', to remind us that there is something other than 'fast food'. It has helped to limit the number of new McDonald's in Italy. There have been other initiatives of the same type in Rome, and also in Venice, with Maurice Béjart as their leader. The famous choreographer supported us right from the beginning during the Millau affair. When I was in prison in Villeneuve-les-Maguelonne, Béjart was one of the first to write; he was prepared to pay the fine himself, he said, and, if only he had been younger, he would have done the same thing himself. When the appeal was being heard in Montpellier, he arrived for the end of the rally. It is a nice illustration of how protests can be understood by people from every social milieu.

I met the leaders of 'Slow Food' last year, when they came to see me on my farm, and I believe that their activities are helping to make people aware of the cultural dimension of food and of cooking. During the Seattle Counter-Summit, products of artisanal manufacture from all over the world were laid out on tables for everyone to taste. By recognizing the value of such produce, we bring together the most diverse peoples.

16 Agriculture is Humanism

José Bové has been credited with libertarian ideas in his youth, but his actions are always constructive; his aim is to reconstruct agriculture by reintegrating it into society.

The cliché of black flags and bomb throwing is a caricature of libertarian thinking. The libertarian is a philosopher, and he poses the key question for a society: 'Are we building an authoritarian or a non-authoritarian world?' The search for an answer to this question engendered the passionate debates and conflicts of the First International. Joseph Proudhon was the first French libertarian thinker. He has been largely forgotten because he fell foul of Karl Marx, but he is nevertheless the father of the co-operative movement in France. All over the country, there are streets named after Elisée Reclus, who was one of the principal thinkers of the libertarian movement. His vision of human geography was rooted in his ideas about the individual and communities, and how they could be reconciled. It is to another libertarian that we owe the slogan: 'Anarchy is the highest expression of order.'

The point is not to live outside society but to build a society that is not based on a system of hierarchic power, one in which each individual is responsible for the liberty of others. Contrary to the old Republican adage 'Liberty ends where it encroaches on that of another', which to my mind has had its day, the libertarian says: 'The more others are free, the more I too become free': the freedom of others is mine to infinity. This strikes me as a magnificent idea. If whoever faces me acquires new rights, I enjoy my own all the more. This type of individualism is at opposite poles from the restrictive vision based uniquely on cohabitation rather than on interaction between people. If we confine ourselves to the maxim 'Liberty ends where that of another begins', we are erecting a barrier, and everyone is free in their own home . . . to quarrel with their neighbours. Frontiers cause wars.

The libertarian philosophical culture is not at all nihilistic. It is mistaken to claim that it leads to a rejection of all structure and all organization. I have never demanded the abolition of multinational institutions at the international level; what I have demanded is their reconstruction on the basis of human rights, both individual and collective.

In Spain, before 1936, an important trade union movement, the Confederacion Nacional del Trabajo (National Labour Confederation), was created around a critique of all systems of vertical power. It was as successful in the countryside as in the towns. We hear plenty about the Spanish Civil War today, but little about the Spanish Revolution or all that was happening in the countryside between 1936 and 1939: collective experiments, land management, village communities created by the Spanish peasants themselves. Interestingly, these libertarian ideas are found in the Zapata plan. And today the Zapatista Movement of Marcos is influenced by the same ideas. In Russia, similar peasant movements emerged in opposition to tsarism, and then to the Red Army, which destroyed them. But half of the Ukraine was liberated by peasant village communities, which organized, federated and fought first against the White Russians and then against the Reds. The leader of this movement spent the last years of his life at Levallois-Perret, where he died in 1934.

The rural world has a non-authoritarian tradition of collectively organized villages. It has emerged historically in completely different parts of the world without any contact between its initiators. How are we to explain this hotbed of libertarianism in rural areas, still visible today? The culture of rural life is first and foremost a culture of sharing. The peasants themselves are in the best position to organize the distribution of the land. Before mechanization, they relied on this basic piece of common sense: there is no point in having more land than you can work in a day. Their calculation was based on the number of working days, the number of people in the family, the number of workers, and the number of persons to be fed. There has always been this tradition of bonds and of equitable distribution, in Russia, Mexico and elsewhere, including France in 1789. In this rural culture, where the land is seen as being there to provide a living and to provide food, there is inevitably a notion of sharing that takes precedence over notions of appropriation or accumulation. If the peasant movement in Russia was destroyed, and if Stalin wanted to liquidate the peasantry with the great famine of

1931–4 in the Ukraine – an organized famine – it is because this type of village community would oppose head-on an attempt to dominate.

What Marx was to the Workers' International, Proudhon could have been to a Peasant International. Are we seeing a swing of the historical pendulum?

We are at all events seeing an international reawakening and a desire for fair shares in the rural world. Through Via Campesina, the association of peasant farmers all over the world now incarnates a resistance that is rooted in places where people live and want their localities to survive. This movement is perhaps emblematic of a new way of re-localizing people's economies and their lives. The point is not to deny that an international organization is necessary, but to demand that it respects the principles enunciated above. Whatever the current disillusion and despair, the social regeneration based on the desire of individuals to take charge of their own destinies might at last, and wholly in accord with historical rural culture, give rise to the international agrarian community.

The peasant struggle incarnates a new citizenship that combines the local and the global. If civil society can identify with the battle of the peasant movement, it is because its themes have a universality that speaks not only to the world's peasants but also to the populations of its towns.

Farmers do not only cultivate the land; they also cultivate human values, perhaps more so than those in other occupations.

The work of the farmer fosters an authentic relationship with nature and with the world, which is as good as any philosophy. I condemn the productivist system for having tried to distance farmers from this relationship to the world, and to reduce them to the performance of technical operations without being required to think about the consequences these might have for the biological equilibrium, the environment, the groundwater or, indeed, social relations. Go on expanding, they were told, what does it matter if this means a neighbour goes under? To dehumanize the farmer's job is to destroy solidarity. Nothing is more disastrous than to transform a peasant farmer into an individualist. Over and beyond the great agricultural debate, farming is a form of humanism.

17 How to Teach Children about Farming

In 2002, for the second year running, the Salon de l'Agriculture organized its publicity campaign round the slogan: 'Bring your family to visit the biggest farm in France.'

We are light years away from education and school camps. We already have Disneyland; now, once a year, we have Agriland.

Behind the scenes, behind the spectacle, the records, the results and the demonstrations of power in the form of massive bulls and huge machines, agribusiness is busy signing contracts. The livestock farmer who has brought his bull has already sold 400 shots of semen.

Any citizens who visit the show hoping to learn more about the problems of small farmers come away even more out of touch with the realities of rural life.

Some schoolchildren who visit François Dufour's farm are given a glimpse of reality.

At the end of March 2001, seventy children from a Poissy secondary school visited my farm. They included many second-generation North Africans and kids of very different backgrounds. They had come not for a course in agricultural technology, but to discover a farm. After a short talk on our various activities, lasting only a quarter of an hour, they were each given a large plateful of rice pudding made by my wife, Françoise, and a choice of apple juice, cider or milk from our cow to drink. Some of the little Moroccan boys drank half a litre straight from the bottle. They took photos of each other sitting on the tractor or the horse, or leading calves by the nose. They were city kids. They spent two hours on the farm, and then we took them to the orchard. At each stop, I avoided too many technical explanations in favour of allowing time for direct contact and practical demonstrations. I told them how to plant a tree, what time of year it flowered, the date of the harvest, the correct time for pruning, and how trees are protected. The teachers who accompanied the children wrote to tell us that the visit had stirred old memories. Two of them telephoned to thank us. They told us what a lot we had taught the children in a short time, and that when they had asked what the children wanted to do on the next school trip, most of them had said: 'Can we spend a whole day on the farm?'

This is one way in which contacts between children of school age and farmers can be developed in natural surroundings, on the farm itself. As I have connections with Morocco, I paid particular attention to the two young Berbers who drank milk because they didn't want cider, an alcoholic drink. They had noticed that we had a campsite, and said they would come to stay there next summer because they wanted to spend a few days in our company. They asked questions about mad cow disease, foot-and-mouth disease, and sheep, having been upset by the scenes of slaughter they had seen over and over again on the television. 'Why did no one cure them?' they asked. And 'Does it mean that now, when you have a sick animal, you kill it and burn it?' They had been deeply affected.

There are several stages to such an education: first the farm visit; then, on a larger scale, the village; lastly the region. It can be approached in a number of ways. School classes can be taken to visit a farm. Or a family can explore regional specialities in the holidays or at exhibitions of local farm produce. The school syllabus needs to be revised; the teaching of French history, for example, could bring a little more immediacy to the question of peasant life, away from eco-museums and temporary exhibitions. As early as infant school, it might be worth starting a vegetable patch. Such schools often own a few animals, but the experience of sowing seed and watching vegetables grow is not common enough. School courses put insufficient emphasis on the extent to which everything starts from plants, and this origin of life has been neglected. City schoolchildren should be taught that without plants there is no animal life. Animals depend on the grasses and the trees.

The weather is a constant preoccupation for many people, but their interest rarely extends beyond the weekend weather forecasts. These could be used as occasions for informing them about the implications for farmers, and the farming calendar, and for reminding them which fruit and vegetables are currently in season. They could be told that the tomatoes or strawberries they see in the shops in December cannot have come from France. They could be warned that if a day comes when they find themselves eating French strawberries at Christmas, it will be because the fruit have been injected with fish genes; since the fish doesn't freeze, neither will the strawberries. Children have little grasp of the cycles of biological life since no one now tells them about seasonal products, the southern winter, the temperate hemisphere, or the consequences of too mild a winter or too wet a summer.

Children need to be taught, or reminded, how the land regulates itself during the course of the year, what happens in the sky with the revolutions of the sun, but also how the land recovers when left to itself. They need to be taught that the rebirth of spring is dependent on what happens in winter, and to be told what goes on in the bare soil or beneath the snow. The soil needs to rest, just as human beings need to rest, for its energy to be restored, so that it is again 'in good heart'. What does this mean? It means being ready to produce once more, but also being capable of withstanding all assaults, such as from plagues of insects, and the vagaries of the climate. If the soil is exhausted, it needs a helping hand, but this does not have to be chemical.

Children ought also to be taught about hedges: that they act as a barrier against erosion, but also provide a habitat for the small animals that are necessary to plant life. If all weeds are systematically killed, all hedge life is killed too. When hedges are restored, dragonflies reappear, and plants that had disappeared from the meadows begin to grow again. Where there are neither hedgerows nor woodland, even an ancient meadow will not regenerate itself, in the absence of that equilibrium in which each insect has its role. It is often the 'pests' that maintain the balance because it is the predators who clean up. It should be explained to children that we are depriving ourselves of our natural defences by sterilizing everything in sight and banishing smells, dust and pollen. Plants need them every day, just as they need the vitamins provided by the sun every day, if they are not to be deprived of minerals.

Children should also be told about the role of bees in the production of honey and legumes. If bees did not carry the fertilizing pollen, what would happen to the apple harvest, or the harvests of strawberries or alfalfa? When hives are placed near to orchards, yields increase by 20 to 30 per cent. This is currently a cause for concern, as the number of bees seems to be in decline. Pollution due to the abuse of insecticides is one of the causes.

For children who eat only fish fingers bought from the supermarket, a fish has neither a head nor a tail, and its real shape remains a mystery. Foods are so highly processed that they can be bought and eaten without any awareness of their relation to farming. In the shops, there is nothing to show that they have been produced on a farm. At this stage, they are simply an industrial or commercial product. How many young school-leavers know that cereals can grow in fields only if the soil contains the humus that is indispensable to all growth? Or that originally, farms had animals that produced milk and meat to feed the family, but also dung that was collected and in due course dug into the soil, that this was enriched by the natural elements in the excrement, and that it was this process that enabled new crops to be grown that would themselves be fed to the beasts?

I believe it is important for schoolchildren to understand this cycle. But when children leave Paris for the provinces, what do they see? Endless fields of cereals or fodder crops, stretching for hundreds of kilometres. Hardly any cattle are visible, and the role of animal manure is a closed book. The only animals they are familiar with are those kept in zoos. For them, animals are simply an attraction that you pay to go and see, maintained by some company that puts them on display for the general public. If they never see them in their natural surroundings, children will have no idea what farming consists of or what values it embodies.

I have made a campsite on my farm. We get a lot of Dutch and Danish visitors who come from towns, and their children come into the mistal during milking. I always keep a mug handy so that I can squeeze the teat and expel some milk for them to drink. These are children who have never been close to a cow before, and whose parents would be incapable of explaining lactation to them. It is an opportunity for me to teach them that it is partly linked to the circulation of the blood and that if the cow hasn't calved, it doesn't produce milk. These little children are quite likely to believe that milk is produced in the cartons their mother buys from the supermarket.

Their farm holiday is also an opportunity to teach them that the quality of the cow's milk depends on the feed she has been given; to make my point, I tell them about the new-born calves that cannot tolerate their mother's milk because the cows have been reared by industrial methods and given stimulants to increase their milk yields.

When they buy cartons of milk, mothers are reassured by the word 'pasteurized'. Fewer and fewer households now drink milk in its raw state. I explain to my visitors that it is simply not true that pasteurized milk is more easily digestible and that it is less stable the minute it is removed from the refrigerator. Pasteurization was introduced to deal with the problems of keeping milk and transporting it over increasingly long distances. It has served as an antidote to production methods that are ever more intensive. It is a way of eliminating risk. It is clear that when you keep cows at a density of several animals per square metre in an industrial shed, the health risks are greatly increased. The response has been, at one end of the process, to add antibiotics to the animal feed and, at the other, to pasteurize the dairy products. The industry has gradually increased its hold on both farmers and consumers and deployed all its technical skills to find ways of protecting it against epidemics, accidents during transport, and breakdowns in the cold chain. In parallel, the politicians have instituted an arsenal of draconian regulations to ensure the safety of products that are dangerous because they are weakened and made to circulate without frontiers or barriers. The CAP and the WTO oblige the governments of rich countries to play the role of firefighters, struggling to cope with the frequency and scale of the disasters they face.

Thus the systematic slaughter of herds of cattle does not stop the prion from spreading, any more than pasteurization prevents cheese from containing listeria.

Informed consumers cannot ignore these risks, which are hidden from them on the pretext of not spreading panic among the public at large. The same governments that are so anxious not to revive old and – allegedly – unjustified fears are nevertheless quite prepared to encourage food phobias in the name of a distorted version of the precautionary principle. This principle is valuable when it is applied to the authorization of new products that may or may not be innocuous, but it is perverted when it is used to justify reassuring the public during epidemics for which the government bears its share of responsibility and whose causes it is reluctant to remedy.

The education of taste is another major area that needs to be addressed. People need to be taught, for example, what a proper carrot tastes like.

If you give young people a carrot that has been grown in a garden with the aid of plenty of good horse muck or garden compost, they are not going to like it. An organic carrot tends to be on the hard side and crunchy. They prefer the chemical carrot that is stuffed full of antibiotics and watery, but much softer, which is what they are used to. They have the same reaction to meat; the bones of a farm rabbit or chicken are harder and the meat is denser; it is also much more nourishing.

But a child who is not used to chewing and digesting meat of this sort is going to find it strange and hard.

Little purpose is served by taking young children out to farms to watch through a glass window as cows are milked by machine, if they don't understand the whole process of rearing livestock: what an animal is, what it eats, where it comes from, what function it serves, and what values it embodies. This is why we are hostile to the museum-farms located close to towns.

Children should be taught about agriculture as part of a much wider education in general culture. Our aim should be to teach every citizen the biological processes of the fauna and flora, the life of the soils, the nature of the air, and the content of water and the subsoil, and to give them a grounding in agronomy. Before children are taken to visit farms, they should have acquired this basic understanding. They ought to know in general terms how nature functions and the relation between the countryside and human activity.

François Dufour's campsite has only six places; it is a tiny pilot scheme for an education in the countryside.

My aim is not to say to my campers: 'I have a herd here that produces 10,000 litres of milk per cow; isn't that marvellous?' Even less: 'Aren't you glad you have a farmer like me to provide you with food?' Instead, what I say to them is this: 'Listen; farming is in difficulties; this is what it used to be like, and this is what it ought to become.'

How can farming be taught as part of a general education?

The Ministry of Education ought to regard a minimum of knowledge about agriculture as part of our general culture. Little collections of animals are relatively frequent in nursery or infant schools, but there are very few vegetable plots to show children how to grow, for example, a leek. Anything to do with cooking is also attractive to children. To get them to cook from a recipe is like giving them an enjoyable demonstration or an experiment in physics or chemistry. On one of the stands at the Salon d'Agriculture, schoolchildren were taught how to break an egg and separate the white from the yolk. But these culinary experiences are no substitute for the experience of having planted seed and then harvested it.

We need to give such an education an institutional dimension so that practical work is rehabilitated at all levels. In many parts of

Norway, agricultural schools are now quite common; a parcel of land on a nearby farm is reserved for the instruction of schoolchildren. The link with nature can begin to be forged at school. Why not draw on the Scandinavian example and introduce into France, during the primary and secondary stages, these practical open-air activities? It would cost the nation very little to make it compulsory for young people to spend three or four days in the country during the course of the school year. We are not talking about exchanges between schools or colleges in rural areas and towns, or about visits to eco-museums or so-called educational farms; what we have in mind is a few days spent on an ordinary working farm. A half-day is not enough.

If we do nothing, our citizens will become even more cut off from agriculture, and also from biodiversity, the countryside and life. As part of the school syllabus, it would be worth organizing a two-pronged approach, browsing on the Internet and practical experience on the ground; it would have to be compulsory, not optional.

A proposal to give a folkloric tinge to a new series of 'Loft Story' (the French 'Big Brother') by setting it in an old-style farm seems to me quite outrageous. The very idea of making a group of young Europeans live like nineteenth-century peasants for the benefit of the cameras is insulting to the hundreds of millions of our contemporaries obliged to live in such conditions today. I was in sympathy with the demonstrators who occupied the film set to protest against this intolerable 'retro' parody. Television is not fulfilling its educational role. With programmes like this, it is even harmful, and it is impeding our efforts to relocate farming within modern society.

18 The Duties of Public Research

The destruction of transgenic rice plants destined for transplanting in the Camargue initiated the GMO trial in the spring of 2001. It had been emergency action taken to prevent them spreading in the atmosphere, explained José Bové, summoned before the high court in Montpellier. But this preventive action, taken in the public interest, was interpreted by those representing the laboratory concerned as an assault on the freedom of research. Lacking technical arguments to prove that the experiment presented no risk to public health, the prosecution tried in vain to imply that this was some sort of medieval trial of science and progress. But both inside and outside the court, in a forum chosen by the campaigners, a great debate had begun on the mission and purpose of research, which has currently lost its way.

This debate was a first. We were able to gain the moral high ground thanks to an ill-advised trial which attempted to dismiss a legitimate act performed in the public interest as a piece of unjustified vandalism. The laboratory (CIRAD) that had started proceedings in association with the public prosecutor found itself in an impasse. It had not been difficult to demonstrate the urgency of our action, as the experimental plants had already been packaged ready to be sent to the Camargue, where they were to be transplanted. But the local rice growers had opposed this, and a prohibition on planting these GMOs had been notified to the senders. There is some uncertainty about the date the document was signed, but these GMOs were doomed in advance not to be used. Two precautionary measures are safer than one.

And we had not been mistaken in our target. Public opinion is hostile to field trials.

The real question was posed at the beginning of the trial, and it was this that legitimized our action. In recent years, the scientific world has operated behind closed doors, hidden away in its ivory tower. We wanted to denounce the way in which scientists have cut themselves off from social reality and from all the problems posed in particular by genetic manipulation, which is putting public health and biodiversity at risk.

Research in molecular biology has been hijacked by productivism. It has not escaped the perversion that has been so destructive of agriculture in general. In receipt of funds from multinational corporations, public laboratories have become satellites in the orbit of the relentless advance of commercialization. There has been confusion, not to say collusion, between public and private research. In France, state-subsidized laboratories have entered the race for advanced technologies, justifying themselves on the grounds that they would be left behind by researchers in America and Japan if they did otherwise.

As a result, they have abandoned programmes that were properly within their competence and might eventually have proved extremely valuable to a sustainable agriculture that paid more respect to the natural cycles and the environment than to an ill-controlled industrialization.

The technocrats who have a supportive advisor in the private offices of ministers have persuaded scientists to take up the gauntlet: 'This is a battle we are not going to lose.' The aim ('to feed the planet') is no longer the purpose of the research. Technology has become an end in itself. The only ethic is the 'new', and we have technological progress for its own sake; it is almost like a religious cult. Technology must be pushed to the limit because new things are learned. Public research is spinning out of control.

To develop transgenic technology as a good in itself, in the hope of a solution to world hunger, is an illusion. GM seeds are not intended for peasants practising subsistence farming. They are for the benefit of the large-scale cereal farmers who are actually killing off local small-scale farming; they are for the big producers who use seeds patented in favour of one or other of the five big companies which are locked in fierce competition and are usurping the right to food sovereignty of the peoples of the developing countries.

The value of the trials, furthermore, does not bear analysis. The technical arguments are unconvincing. It is claimed, for example, that it is essential for trials to be conducted out in the open and not under glass. This is to test their dissemination, at the stage preceding use. But pollen does not need to be transgenic to circulate, and it would be quite possible to test the potential propagation of the genes with non-transgenic plants, so that separation distances could be established and the size of the necessary buffer zones determined . . . or the impossibility of any certainty revealed.

It is well known that rape seed is extremely volatile. It is hardly necessary to plant a GMO to know how many kilometres the pollen can travel, or whether birds and insects come into contact with it. Cross-pollination can be studied in a glasshouse. Such studies exist.

But the big question is this: so far, we have proceeded with the manipulation of genes in the dark. We know how to modify them, but not how this happens in the life cycle and in an ecosystem; we lack the parameters to measure all the repercussions, once they are dispersed. When you modify a living thing, you lose control. What chain of consequences will follow from the cross-pollination of GMOs with wild species? What sort of pollution may be caused in identical but untreated species, which will themselves be transformed? We await precise replies.

Researchers ask us if we are fundamentally opposed in principle to genetic research. It is not a matter of being dogmatically for or against, but of being pragmatic. We are asking for field trials to be abandoned because they serve no purpose and because they are dangerous. Such a prohibition would not slow down fundamental research; it would also encourage some hard thinking about the true priorities of research and clearer definitions of the different spheres of competence of the private and the public, whose aims are opposed. It is important that those engaged in research act with greater transparency and take account of social realities. What is their function? It is not to put the organization of science at the heart of society, which would be to return to the positivism of the nineteenth century.

Livestock breeders have shown that there is no need to have recourse to genetic manipulation to select according to quality; they have been successful in improving the quality of cattle by cross-breeding. The work carried out by the Institut National de la Recherche Agronomique (National Institute for Agronomic Research) on flocks of ewes, in particular those of the Larzac, has been satisfactory in the case both of milk production and of lambing.

Why should we not develop agronomic methods for plants as for animals? Why struggle to prove the necessity of creating transgenic plants, when the complexity of the parameters is even less controllable?

As for the argument that they will improve yields and provide better nutrition for populations that are short of food, the case is far from proven. Sufficient resources exist to feed the planet. Agronomy has demonstrated the efficiency of agricultural practices that were wasteful neither of energy nor of fossil fuels, posed no danger to the environment, and yet produced yields that stand up to all comparison. More work could be done to improve these methods.

Manufacturing plants that are herbicide pumps, or plants to produce an insecticide, a colza that is three times more resistant, or beet in the maize fields, serves only to increase the performance of intensive agriculture in the short term; it does nothing to achieve sustainable agricultural growth. Even the results, what is more, are by no means guaranteed. The GMO crops grown in the United States have not led to any varietal improvement.

The motives of those in favour of GMO plants are not humanitarian, even if that is how they are dressed up; nor are they economically advantageous for the community as a whole (all costs compared). They are motivated solely by financial gain. GMOs would not be viable if it was not the intention of the companies seeking to market them to make them patentable. Their only interest is in the profit of owning the patent.

Researchers are becoming more aware of these issues. The involvement of INRA in Genoplante has been questioned. It is aberrant that publicly funded research should participate in work that is intended to enable companies to enter the race for patents in living things. The purpose of science is to understand life. The manufacture of GMOs has nothing to do with knowledge of living things. Public research has better things to do than collaborate in the privatization of a genetic patrimony that belongs to humanity.

How can research workers in specialized fields accept that people are attempting to pass off as scientific something that is not? Only if they remain within a closed circle and take no notice of the outside world, and only if they refuse to speak to anyone who is not an expert, can they any longer remain indifferent to the particular manipulations to which they are subject as soon as a market depends on the results of their research; in this case, the potential market is that in the control of genes.

In the productivist logic, as soon as a technical means exists, it is exploited to the full without thought for its impact. What does it matter if there is a risk of cross-allergy caused by the spread of transgenic pollen? In any case, if any damage is done, some technological whiz kid will be there to sort it out. The scientists, from whom we expect above all expertise, can no longer shirk their responsibilities, or avoid entering into a dialogue with the citizens who have a right to take part in the debate, though it has been denied them for fifty years.

The history of antibiotics ought to make us more cautious with regard to transgenic products. Once a remedy called on in an emergency, antibiotics are now routinely used to reassure, and on a massive scale. And as if that were not enough, they are now being misused. Today, in the United States, 70 per cent of antibiotics are produced not to treat humans but to dope healthy animals. They are used not as an anti-bacterial agent but as a growth-promoter. They are administered to cattle so that their milk and meat production is speeded up. Europe is following suit.

If these products are used in pots of baby food, will this state-of-the-art veterinary medicine shrug its shoulders and say 'Not my problem'?

Hybridization was an early form of industrialization, with its aim being the privatization of seeds. It was said to be the best way of improving the production of maize. The process was perfected in the 1910s. It was a myth; the truth is that its use forced farmers to buy fresh seed every year. For the first time the big groups imposed market logic on the right to sow. GMOs are only a further stage in the process by which the seed merchants are gaining control, the apotheosis of a process that began with the hybrids.

The new mystification is to justify experiments with GMOs by brandishing the alibi of world famine. The seed firms call for the support of researchers by dangling the prospect of the final solution to the problem of world hunger.

Even the FAO has succumbed to the pressure of the food processing industry by accepting the principle of the genetic manipulation of seeds. The final declaration that closed the Rome summit in June 2002 advocates 'reasonable' controls on transgenic crops. We should not be deceived by this formula, with its pretence of 'balance'. The communiqué was drawn up without the debate having taken place. My message to the seed merchants is this: 'You have the hearts of monopolists. But you are not agronomists, able to convince us of the superiority of transgenic colza or soya; nor are you economists, capable of proving that it is only thanks to your patents that nine million people will be fed.'

The seed firms are engaging in a form of ecological blackmail by presenting us with false alternatives: excessive chemistry or GMOs. This is a lie. It is also a lie to claim that the food self-sufficiency of the planet cannot be achieved without recourse to GMOs, or else we will have to go on exhausting the soils. It is the international regulations encouraging dumping, and the policy of subsidizing exports from the rich countries to the poor countries, the invasion of the agricultures of the South by those of the North, that, by the underhand but deliberate action of the lobbies, are preventing the achievement of food self-sufficiency throughout the world. By driving peasant farmers off their burned lands, in Borneo, in the Amazon, and elsewhere, by destroying their market gardens, and by confusing taxation and predation, a scorched-earth policy is being implemented, and the way paved for the reign of those who have patented living things.

Have the researchers nothing to say about the endless crises that are being experienced by the exporting countries?

The famous 'precautionary principle' is the lifebelt of short-sighted ministers. They press the red button that says 'stop everything'. To avoid situations where they have to apply in an emergency, in times of crisis, a maximalist precautionary principle, and traumatize public opinion, they would do well to think ahead; they should be applying the principle of maximum prevention of all the potential risks to which the publicly funded experts have a duty to alert us, independently of all special interests. It is for scientists to reappropriate, as responsible citizens, the precautionary principle that the politicians have borrowed from them and misused for opportunist ends.

Research into the impact of a discovery is increasingly a priority in this spiral of inventions, into which scientists have been sucked. Every technological advance should be analysed in relation to its impact – that is, its effect on the autonomy and creativity of individuals, the social ties it implies, the forms of power it imposes, and its capacity to maintain over the long term a future for the planet.

19 Farming Think Tanks and International Workshops

The reform of the CAP is urgent, but only a palliative. How can the causes of the malaise be addressed, or the deep imbalances corrected, without major structural changes to the decision-making and administrative institutions?

The international tools need to be strengthened by giving some coherence to the institutions.

The WTO claims a vocation to extend its sphere of competence and superior decision-making powers to the whole range of human activities: agriculture, services and intellectual property rights. It is engaged in a bid to organize the world order on the basis of an economic logic with a single ideology.

It is our contention that, on the contrary, the expansion of the WTO must be limited, and a number of areas excluded from its competence: namely, those concerning the food sovereignty of peoples, food safety and biodiversity – that is, the mainstays of agriculture in the sense of the cultivation of living things.

It is not our aim, we should emphasize, to challenge the principle of the organization of trade; free trade is out of the question. Rules are necessary in order to make international trade more transparent and more equitable, and to fight illicit agreements, cartels, clandestine trade and dumping.

We are convinced that it would be more appropriate for matters such as agriculture and food, public health and the environment, the preservation of natural resources, the soil, the water and the air, and the risks of pollution to come within the remit of the FAO; this organ of the United Nations is best qualified to act as arbiter and guarantor in such matters.

All disputes of an economic and social nature that arise between states, or bring individuals and transnational groups into conflict, should come within the remit of a judicial institution that is independent of the WTO itself. The system that gives the WTO the privilege of having its own internal mechanism for settling disputes is wholly perverse. There is no facility for any external appeal against its rulings. Independence and democracy would be better served if this arbitration were under the aegis of the United Nations, an institution in whose decision making every country has a voice.

In the same way that the general condemnation of impunity with regard to war crimes against humanity eventually forced democratic governments to set up an International Court of Criminal Justice (the United States signed after the others but has never ratified it), the defence of economic and social rights ought to have its equivalent: an independent appeals structure that would operate in the general interest on the basis of written law and not the case law established by the WTO.

This law would override market logic; it would enable legal action to be taken against abuses of power and against regulations that ran counter to the fundamental texts, whether the economic, social and cultural pacts agreed by the member states in 1966, which recognize the right to food, shelter, work, culture and education, or a rider to the Universal Declaration of Human Rights. This new document might complement the declaration as regards a sustainable farming that conformed to a common charter and was based on a set of conditions defining the rights and duties of the peasant farmer as citizen and consumer. These new modernizing texts could be submitted for the approval of the member states of the United Nations.

If the International Court were to condemn a state or a multinational for a blatant violation of social or environmental ethics, or for endangering natural resources, the common property of humanity, the problem of imposing the penalty would remain. Today, apart from diplomatic censure unaccompanied by action, who can compel the United States to reduce its level of greenhouse gas emissions? Who can oblige the occupant of the White House to pay the eco-tax in his capacity as polluter of the planet? At present, unbending in their disdainful refusal, the American government is untouchable.

When disputes come before the court of the WTO, it is always the stronger country that penalizes the weaker. If Costa Rica, for example, or Haiti were to be successful in a case concerning pollution or imbalances, they have no means of forcing the United States or Europe to submit.

The American decision to increase grants of federal aid to farmers by 70 per cent in ten years is in contravention of the commitments made at the WTO conference in Doha in November 2001. At home, the United States fails to practise what it preaches (the abolition of subsidies); in fact, it does exactly the opposite. The new Farm Bill reveals the hypocrisy of the Bush administration, which does not itself abide by the rules it seeks to impose on the world market. If protectionist measures taken by a government ruin the local economies of Southern countries, what new international jurisdiction will punish it?

It is essential, therefore, that we change the balance of power so that international regulations are applied in full in the interests of the community as a whole and not imposed by the strongest on the weakest. Some specialists in international commercial law are considering the possibility of snaring the greatest superpower in a new judicial net if it refuses to pay for its pollution, placing itself above the law. If a state refuses to sign a treaty that is agreed by the majority of states and that affects the living conditions of people living on the land, legal proceedings might be instituted against persons with direct moral responsibility for the excessive greenhouse gas emissions; they might be sentenced to pay the eco-tax and fines: for example, the oil companies, the automobile firms and the chemical industries.

The counter-summit to the Johannesburg Earth Summit of 2002 reignited the debate about how to convince the greatest world power to abandon its ecological isolationism and economic exceptionalism when the Earth's environment is in danger.

In the case of France and Europe, the very structure of the various ministries of agriculture has demonstrated an inability to prevent the crises, appreciate the true priorities, stop playing 'divide and rule' with regard to the farming world, pursue a coherent policy, or see problems in their wider context: jobs, health, training, diversity and living conditions.

In France, joint management with the largest union has had its day. It is no more than a pale shadow of a policy; it reduces the minister to a sort of administrative dinosaur and registry office. The government should stop counting farmers and flattering them in their capacity as voters and start consulting them as citizens, all equal in rights and duties. It is high time they ceased separating producers and consumers.

One can envisage a Ministry of Agriculture and Food Safety which, shorn of its lobbies and all those accountants now permanently occupied doling out subsidies, might be a tool capable of responding to the demands of a coherent, sustainable and fair policy; it would be important, however, to avoid falling into the trap of a super-ministry and attempting to absorb Environment, already attached to National and Regional Development. To put food under the aegis of the Minister of Agriculture, as happened with the formation of the new government after the presidential election of May 2002, is a gesture in the direction of the consumer, but does nothing to solve the problem of reshaping the management of French agricultural policy.

A think tank on trade union representation would be useful. The decision-makers of the FNSEA, cut off from their base, are no longer men of the soil, but have their fingers in many pies. The ordinary citizen ought to be aware that the members of the Board of Directors of the FNSEA are also presidents of the Crédit Agricole, Groupama and the MSA – that is, the three largest co-operatives in France. They are also presidents of the Offices created by Michel Rocard, Minister for Agriculture at the beginning of the 1980s. These act as intermediaries between the government and the various production chains, each of which has its own Office: Onilait for milk, Oliflor for flowers and horticulture, Onivin for viticulture, Ofival for meat, and Onipam for aromatic and medicinal plants. Each Office has a budget and is presided over by a member of the FNSEA. Joint management is thus pretty comprehensively tied up in a sort of secular pluralism. All the farmer can do is implement the directives handed down from above. If Education is an elephant in need of a drastic slimming down, Agriculture is an octopus very badly in need of having its tentacles hacked off.

How is this to be done? We should start at the bottom, establishing committees in every canton that would be chaired by an elected official such as a mayor or municipal councillor. One or two members per farming union should be appointed to the committee, together with delegates from rural development, nature preservation and consumer groups. Brought out into the open like this, farming would be put back in touch with society.

Urging citizens to feel greater solidarity with those who provide their food does not mean creating extra drought, flood and epidemic taxes. Why not a farming tax taken from VAT? This would have to be ratified and standardized at the European level. What could be more effective than a campaign for transparency with regard to the true costs of production and proper remuneration for the value added by the peasant farmer?

The way the countryside should be utilized remains a major preoccupation. When the land loses its function as a provider of food, thanks to the expansion of off-soil 'farming', the countryside risks being seen as a sort of open-air museum, or leisure park, with a little niche production and a few model villages. A safeguard should be built in to the land register: the obligation to maintain in perpetuity a certain percentage of cultivated land within a defined area. All mayors refer to the famous Plan d'Occupation des Sols, or 'plan for land use' in their commune. One can envisage a Plan d'Occupation de la Campagne, or 'plan for countryside use', which would ensure that a sufficient area was set aside for farming to be able to continue with its prime function and its many associated tasks: the shaping of the landscape, the prevention of desertification and soil degradation, and a respect for resources and the environment. But this plan would have to be accompanied by a document spelling out what methods of cultivation could be used. It would be more difficult to adapt the Plan d'Occupation des Sols to demographic change in the less advanced countries, a pressing issue for the world's billion and a half country-dwellers.

20 The Pillars of Peasant Wisdom

Is a Pax Romana on the basis of a Charter agreed by all parties, even old enemies, possible? Or will there have to be a 'Carnation Revolution', or rather a 'Daisy Revolution', called after the flower that is the emblem of the Confédération Paysanne? Each petal of this flower represents an activity that helps to maintain a balance in the way a farm is run.

We chose the daisy primarily because it is a wild flower. The harmony of the flower depends on the petals; if one is removed, the flower loses all its beauty. We chose this image to make the point that peasant farming is a whole, a collection of interrelated parts, like petals, and that the removal of just one element unbalances the whole enterprise.

Let us take as an example the so-called precision farming (*agriculture raisonée*), which uses fewer chemical fertilizers, or even organic farming, which uses none at all. If one farm of this type corners rights to produce in the sphere of dairy, pig or poultry farming, it creates an imbalance in the number of jobs in relation to volume of production (work-load per hectare). This type of agriculture, even organic, which would respect the environment, would nevertheless be a form of industrial agriculture because it destroyed jobs in its sector.

Another petal of the daisy symbolizes the possibility of the farm being transmitted to others. This transmissibility depends on the size, the investment, and the balance between production and the tools of production on the farm. Let us postulate a highly mechanized farm, worked by only one man, with an automatic milking machine, worth five or six million francs at handover; there is no way it can be taken over in the normal way or that jobs can be created at a normal cost.

Another petal represents the autonomy of the farm that is not dependent on massive imports of products from outside.

Next comes the capacity of the farm to provide a decent living income on the basis of an acceptable work-load for all involved. When a small farm cannot provide a sufficient income, it may be that processing could enable it to release extra value and create additional employment. This is another aspect to be borne in mind in seeking to restore harmony to the 'daisy'. Ways of adapting or strengthening this or that aspect of peasant farming can be devised.

It would be useful to introduce the issue of farm viability, with reference to all these aspects, into the syllabus of the agricultural schools where young people are trained. Within the context of the reconversion of farms, it might be possible to persuade farmers to take all these criteria into account and not only the single economic criterion of maximizing subsidies and running the farm in whatever way attracts the largest share of the steady stream of handouts emanating from Brussels.

How does small-scale farming relate to 'precision farming'?

'Precision farming' is one of the great myths of recent years. It is an attempt to paint productivism in 'green' colours by suggesting that reducing or rationalizing the use of pesticides and chemical fertilizers is enough to remedy the current imbalances in agricultural production.

'Precision farming' is a way of keeping the current system going by means of sleight of hand. It is agribusiness's 'certificate of good conduct', the green façade of the FNSEA. It was endorsed by the government decree of 25 April 2002, its official recognition a sure sign that joint management of farming by union and ministry is alive and well.

In this review of the ten founding principles of peasant farming, José Bové notes the first examples of their application on the ground, or, where this is not yet the case, suggests what might be done.

Principle 1: to redistribute volumes of production to allow as many people as possible to enter farming and earn a living from it.

A redistribution of this type was implemented in the case of Roquefort when it was decided that every producer had the right to produce 350 hectolitres of milk per farm so as to be assured of a minimum income. This is contrary to the policy of quotas, where the quantity allocated to each individual remains fixed until the end of their days. By imposing limits on those who had the largest quotas, adequate quotas were ensured for the less well off. This is a fair scheme that ought to be extended to other forms of production organized at the

European level. It is a concrete example of what can be achieved in the case of a local product when power is held locally.

Principle 2: to show solidarity with small farmers in other parts of Europe and all over the world.

This principle is now being applied in the Fair Trade movement; also in the production of vegetable proteins at home, so that the farmers of Southern countries are not obliged to grow raw materials for the export market; and also by restricting production so as not to end up exporting at dumping prices – that is, by not running one's farm on the basis of the export logic.

Principle 3: to respect nature.

Here, there is no shortage of examples. They include stopping the ensilage of maize and the use of soya, and converting the fields freed up into meadows of mixed grasses and nitrogenous legumes, so ensuring a coherent balance on the farm.

Principle 4: to make the best of abundant resources and conserve scarce resources.

Human resources are not in short supply among rural populations. Better use could be made of them if they were employed in acceptable social conditions. The labour of the farmer that creates added value should be remunerated at its true worth. The capital contribution, on the other hand, is a resource that is not easily renewable. It is unfair when the over-provision of equipment and the cost of supplies leads to job losses or when the repayment of credit swallows up much of the reward for labour.

Every time that a new farmer is spared having to buy land, a scarce resource is husbanded, and the creative value of work recognized. Every time that the volume of external purchases on a farm is reduced, or less is borrowed for capital investment, this principle is being respected.

Principle 5: to be transparent in the activities of buying, producing and selling agricultural produce.

Traceability requires detailed schedules to specify methods of production and record in detail how the animals have been fed and what commitments have been made by the producer. This sort of precise information is provided in the case of organic farming. In the same spirit, associations of farmer-producers who sell directly to the consumer make formal written commitments so that consumers are fully informed about the provenance of the products they are buying.

Buyers are largely ignorant of the difference between farm and dairy products. We have been unable to persuade the Minister of Agriculture to legislate on the concept. We would like the farmer-producer to be identified by a production method, size of workshop, and method of processing that would be defined product by product. We must brace ourselves for a real trial of strength. The battle has been lost in the case of the so-called farm chicken which is nothing more than a label, and here it is too late to turn the clock back. There is a similar problem with Camembert, which has become a generic name. With the exception of AOC Camembert, this cheese can now be made more or less anyhow and anywhere, without any connection to Normandy.

Can you trust the 'red label' quality mark in the case of eggs and poultry?

It offers a sort of guarantee. The specifications are hardly demanding, but it is still a product manufactured according to a contractual agreement. The processor and the producers have made certain undertakings with regard to the number of days the bird is reared, and the number of animals per square metre in the case of chickens, guinea fowl and other birds. One reservation: on the packaging, only the words 'red label' appear, and most people do not know what exactly this means. We would like this information to be given in much more detail so that the consumer can be aware of the realities of the production methods.

Principle 6: to ensure that produce both tastes good and is safe.

Let us take the example of the AOC, where a real effort has been made with regard to safety and taste. Producers are bound by contract to respect regulations that are local, honest and consistent. Through its AOC, the cheese of the Basque country and Béarn retains a special taste and also a link with a locality and a specific type of mountain sheep farming and method of manufacture. The AOC provides protection against the risk of ewes being imported. The cheese in question can only be produced using the milk of the local Pyrenean breeds. This is an excellent example of how a very localized product, long only sold privately, can be developed, and its name made famous, without a loss of its essential qualities. The same can be said of the Reblochon of Haute-Savoie. The public is well able to recognize products of this sort. The possibility of making a choice of farm produce at open-air markets or fairs allows consumers to discover a whole range of flavours. They are also given an opportunity to rediscover old varieties of vegetable, and the chance to taste them on the spot and get advice on cooking them.

It is like a school that provides an education in taste. If you are able to compare an old apple with a Golden Delicious pumped full of water and fertilizer, you will soon learn to tell the difference. There are ten different ways of cooking potatoes. You need a different type of potato for making soup, mash, chips or potato salad. We should stop talking about a product as such. The apple does not exist 'as such', but for a particular quality. If you are making apple sauce, you don't use a cider apple, just as you don't use a cider apple to make an apple tart, and so on. Each specificity in a variety has its own logic. And to make a certain dish, you need to know which type of apple to buy. To the pleasure of recognizing flavours is added the pleasure of naming them. The pleasures of the table include the pleasure of talking about the food you are eating.

Principle 7: to seek maximum autonomy in the way farms are run.

Cereal farmers acquire autonomy as soon as they are in a position to feed their own animals and use their own fertilizer, prepared from their own dung. By reducing as far as possible imports from outside, a balance is achieved between what is produced on the farm and what is needed to produce it. The coherence of a farm derives from the production that is carried out within its boundaries and from the local processing of the produce harvested on it, with the added value.

Principle 8: to seek partnership with other players in the rural world.

The first step is to integrate farms into a social milieu, not run them in isolation. Through their links with artisans they help to create a living community. By the nature of their work farmers provide employment for blacksmiths and mechanics. They also contribute to the maintenance of public services such as schools. Similarly, they keep local open-air markets going, and so bring consumers and producers into direct contact. Farms are also important as places where townspeople can take holidays and where children can be educated.

The Confédération Paysanne has frequently set up 'farms of the future' in town centres, complete with animals; the aim has been to make people think about the future of farming and encourage an ongoing debate between country-dwellers and townspeople. The spirit of partnership develops bonds within the social tissue and new ties of solidarity. Farmers cannot remain aloof from the fate of other social categories. When the railway workers went on strike in November 1995, farmers in many places took them produce, and parties were held with the striking workers in railway stations, complete with barbecues and braziers. They were thus indirectly helping to keep a local station going and stop a public service being dismantled. Such demonstrations of solidarity, over and above trade union rivalries, help build and maintain contacts.

Among the players in the rural world are, of course, the nature conservancy bodies. There is no hostility between farmers and those who care about the environment. This can be seen in a very concrete form in many departments, where action groups have been formed round what is called the 'Alliance', which brings together members of the Confédération Paysanne and local consumer and environmental groups. Petitions have been circulated against the establishment of new industrial pig farms. Here, farmers, environmentalists, consumers and villagers have come together to fight a common battle. The struggle over water is our struggle, too. In Brittany, two years ago, we gave our support to the local group that was protesting against the deterioration in the quality of tap water. The Confédération Paysanne took part in demonstrations alongside consumers of water and it remains on the alert.

Principle 9: to maintain the diversity of livestock reared and plants grown.

People are becoming increasingly aware that local breeds have been developed over time to be adapted to a climatic zone and altitude, to a particular type of pasture, and to a particular type of production that is completely assimilated to the locality. Thus in Aveyron, the Aubrac breed, which had almost disappeared, has been successfully saved and developed. One might also mention the Salers and numerous other breeds that are, happily, still in existence. In the Hautes-Pyrénées, breeds of beef cattle are being developed according to certain strict criteria. Local producers have co-operated in a five-year plan to establish a quality mark for local veal, with a guarantee that the suckling calves have been given only feed produced on the farm. It is a way of demonstrating the coherence of the enterprise. When they say 'we produce our own veal', they are saying far more than that; they are saying that the animals have been given feed composed entirely of produce grown on the farm and so deriving from a fundamental animal/plant balance. Economically, these revivals are viable. These breeds and plants are perfectly adapted to their zones of production and have an excellent natural yield.

Principle 10: to think always in the long term and globally, with an eye to sustainable globalization and growth.

Farmers should have an overall vision and also be able to believe that their farm will endure and be transmitted to future generations. This raises a general question: what procedures are needed to facilitate the transmission of farms? The ideal would be a system that encompassed the whole area, careers and installation on farms as well as modes of transmission. Any such system should extend to include retirement for farmers. Their retirement prospects should be equivalent to those of other social groups, so that they have no need to hang on to some of their buildings and part of their land to be assured of an income.

We now come to sustainable development, recently the subject of an international conference in Johannesburg. We were able to restate our own views. Working for the long term means not exhausting the soils or destroying the land, but maintaining a harmony between the environment and the rural milieu. If the two are in balance, a farm can survive. For example, in areas of bocage the hedges must be preserved, both to prevent erosion and to preserve the habitat of the local fauna. Nor should we forget the other function of these green walls in certain areas – that is, acting as windbreaks and creating within the farm micro-climates that are favourable to particular types of crop. They are also a useful source of timber and firewood.

These are our ten principles. Viticulture in France has experienced a true renaissance by emphasizing quality rather than quantity, especially in the south, and particularly in the Aude and Hérault. To what extent are the wine-growers applying our principles of peasant farming?

Viticulture is in the same situation as farm produce. It has prospered by limiting the number of hectolitres per hectare and by modifying grape varieties with a gain in quality. A number of wine-growers want to go further, in particular in their methods of cultivation; they are seeking to reduce the use of fertilizers and pesticides, which is still on a large scale. A major effort is being made in the case of fertilization, for example, by sowing grass between the rows of vines and making green manure. Others are currently experimenting with the use of old grape varieties from before the phylloxera epidemic.

Young wine-growers are turning to agronomic research in their quest for new qualities and new tastes, in particular the rediscovery of forgotten aromas. They are offering a wide range that encourages us to forget that wines are beginning increasingly to resemble each other. This ongoing research effort is in marked contrast to the standardization produced by some more industrialized wine making, in which genes are introduced into the fermentation. The battle of the wine-growers against the industrializing logic that exists in other fields is in the spirit of the ten principles laid out above.

Vigilance is needed in the face of threats to pervert the AOC system. In the commune of Aniane (Hérault), a big American multinational has been trying to establish itself with the intention of creating a 'wine factory' or 'winery'. Its initial tactic was to buy the wine from the producers in order to break the local co-operative; they would then produce wine in their industrial winery. The project risked destroying the co-operative system by luring away producers, although their collective resulted from a battle early in the twentieth century, in 1907, which led to the creation of the Fédération des Caves Cooperatives. This was a social advance, which had an enormous impact on the structure of rural society. A new battle has been fought in this sector in an attempt to ward off this dangerous project, which seems to be stalled at least for the moment.

Consumers need to be on their guard, not only with regard to the misuse of the 'Vin de pays' appellation but to a whole panoply of misleading labels. When you see table wines labelled 'Vin des communautés européennes' on supermarket shelves at four francs a litre, you feel like serving it to the European Commissioners, the fifteen Ministers of Agriculture, and all the profiteers of the CAP – while yourself enjoying some of the delicious AOC wines that are above suspicion.

21 A Farming Charter and a Declaration of Rights and Duties

Our experience and long consideration reveal both the huge ethical vacuum at the national and international levels and the urgent need to rebuild an activity that is essential but currently heading for disaster. What is needed is a new 'World Charter for Farming'.

The Charter would be based on the 'Six Pillars of Farming Wisdom', which can be summarized as follows:

1 Increasing the number of farms and reducing the concentration of production in Europe and throughout the world.
2 Protecting natural resources and respecting the environment.
3 Rebuilding consumer confidence by ensuring the quality, safety and flavour of products.
4 Reintegrating farming into rural society.
5 Maintaining the diversity of the animal and the plant population.
6 Working for sustainable development.

The Charter proposes a new social contract bringing together farmers and citizens. It concerns all the social partners and all the political representatives. But it will also commit its subscribers to show respect for a number of rules of good social conduct. If we ask the citizen to defend the rights of the farmer, the farmer must accept in return that he or she has obligations to consumers. These reciprocal rights and duties remain to be formulated, as they affect each responsible individual. As we have sketched them below, they could constitute an essential supplement to the Universal Declaration of Human Rights. They might serve as a basis for discussion at future debates and forums.

Universal Declaration of the Rights and Duties of the Farmer and the Citizen

The *farmer* is a countryman or woman of a region and a citizen of the world. This double status confers rights and duties in the context both of their community and of the world as a whole.

- a right to work and fair pay;
- a right to access to the land;
- a right to social status;
- a right to the transmissibility of the patrimony and knowledge;
- a duty towards the regional and world environment;
- a duty towards future generations;
- a duty to all the small farmers of the world and their similar mission to produce food;
- a duty to defend human rights wherever they are threatened;
- a duty to oppose the privatization of the common property of humankind.

The *citizen* is expected to accept the reciprocity of these rights and duties and to include them in the daily exercise of the rights conferred by the Universal Declaration of Human Rights.

The citizen recognizes that farmers perform an indispensable function and that their presence in the countryside is in the public interest.

The citizen opposes a further reduction in the number of farms and the concentration of production.

The citizen is a beneficiary of farming and has a duty to support it. Wishing farming to be well done, the citizen, like the farmer, rejects the notion that it should be subject to the law of the market.

The citizen is supportive of farmers in their difficulties and claims freedom of choice as a consumer and in his or her way of life.

The citizen accepts that farmers should be rewarded for their labour and for the added value of the products they provide.

The citizen recognizes the social status of the farmer and will not accept a situation where farmers are on benefit and treated as employees of private industry or as civil servants assigned to be wardens of national parks.

In return and in exchange:

> Farmers, having recovered their autonomy, will be thrifty with public money.
>
> Citizens have the right to know who are the polluters at every stage in the food chain.
>
> Farmers recognize that their right to use the land does not exempt them from the obligation to respect the soil as a common property of humanity.
>
> Farmers ought to perform their mission to produce food while at the same time protecting natural resources and the environment.
>
> Farmers have a responsibility for biological diversity.
>
> The purpose of agricultural production is not profit but the food sovereignty of the population of the farmer's country or region.
>
> Every farmer stands together with farmers all over the world.

We all have equal rights and equal duties:

> Farmers ought to work for the export market only when this is not detrimental to the food sovereignty of the importing countries.
>
> Farmers should retain the freedom to choose their farming methods, and be free to refuse the directives of a policy that runs counter to their prime mission to provide food or is dictated by pressure groups.
>
> Farmers should serve the community as a whole and not particular interest groups.
>
> Farmers should sell produce that is wholesome, of good quality, and not reserved for privileged groups, but available to the population as a whole, without cultural discrimination or segregation based on income.

Conclusion: The Food War will not Happen

What can French farmers, rooted in the soil but not buried in it, expect from a Republic with feet of clay?

Not, to be sure, a new Gambetta.

The day of the man of the moment is past.

What matters is the political will to get the Declaration of the Rights and Duties of the Farmer and the Citizen accepted and implemented.

Surely the France that produced the Rights of Man cannot be the last country to defend this new charter before the United Nations?

When two worlds do not understand each other, the threat of war is imminent.

Without playing Cassandra, we see looming on the horizon the scenario of an economic world war that would benefit groups competing for hegemony, the hawks who use both biological weapons (epidemics) and psycho-demagoguery ('polluter-farmers', 'freedom of research', 'scientific progress', 'modernity', 'defending the purse of the consumer' and so on).

If education disarms the aggressors, the food war will not happen.

To all the young people who sport the logo 'No future' on their T-shirts, we suggest this new credo: 'The land is my future.'

Let those who would dispute this at least remember the main argument of our book: without farmers, there will be no future.